When Chickens Come Home to Roost

And Other Stories From An International Life

Michael Alford

Cover Design
Gabriela Alford and Justin Luke

ISBN:979-8-8669-2521-6

DEDICATION
To those former colleagues who did good.
You know who you are.

.

Contents

Acknowledgements

Above all, I acknowledge and thank the Office of the United Nations High Commissioner for Refugees (UNHCR) for affording me, and my family, the most amazing work and living experiences. I spent some 40 marvellous years working for the United Nations with exceptional colleagues and in unusual locations. In some jobs, those which are repetitious, it is said, one has 40 times 1 year of experience. In my career, each year, even each month, was a novel experience. For that I am incredibly grateful. I certainly consider myself both lucky and privileged.

I am grateful to the following persons who reviewed one or more of the stories and provided valuable advice: David Alford, Ian Bennet, Uli von Blumenthal, Maricela Daniel, Eddie Gedalof, Malcolm Goodale, Marta Lovisolo, and Astrid Vogel. Final copy-editing was in the very capable hands (keyboard) of Rebecca Alford.

Many thanks to Gabriela Alford and Justin Luke for the design of the cover.

Preface

I spent 32 years of my working life at the Office of the United Nations High Commissioner for Refugees (UNHCR), two at the International Labour Organisation (ILO) and two at the UN System Staff College (UNSSC). I enjoyed postings in Geneva, Canberra, Mogadishu, Hong Kong, Addis Ababa and Tel Aviv with many shorter missions to numerous different locations. After retirement I consulted for five years with a wide range of UN Agencies including WHO, ITU, UNAIDS and UNICEF.

These stories take place in Somalia, Israel, Hong Kong, Iraq and Kenya. The title story and final story are situated in multiple global locations. All build on personal fragments of my experience, and while shaped by my experiences, they are essentially fictitious. That being said, it can be a challenge to distinguish fact from fiction. All characters in these stories derive from my imagination, but what is imagination but a reflection of what might have been, what should have been and what actually was? But please, as you read this, don't try to discern the fact from fiction. At times when writing, even I could not do so.

Many of my colleagues, who have had equally or even more varied and exciting experiences than I, have chosen to write non-fiction accounts of their UN life. I prefer the flexibility of fiction.

All the stories are short, except for the title story, "When Your Chickens Come Home to Roost". While the stories and characters are fictitious, most locations, such as towns, streets, buildings and restaurants are real. In the majority of cases, I have had first-hand experience in these locations.

While fiction, this collection can be considered a substitute for an account of snippets of my working life. So, it is a kind of fictional memoir. At the end of the book, I have recounted some, albeit not all, of the actual events described or alluded to in the stories, which I personally experienced or with which I was directly involved.

In the first and last stories, it may appear that I am critical, or imply criticism of the United Nations. Indeed, I have highlighted, from my personal perspective, many challenges with which the organisation is faced. The UN is by no means perfect, but on balance it does good and is an essential player in global diplomacy, humanitarian affairs, international development and standard setting in a myriad of critical realms. I trust former colleagues familiar with the UN will not feel I am undermining its good works. Equally, I beg that those unfamiliar with the UN, while maybe gaining a better understanding of some aspects of its work, will not come to the conclusion that it is terminally ill.

When Your Chickens Come Home to Roost

Prologue
Contemplation

February 2019

It took me some time and much soul searching to decide whether to relate to you this story. It is an extraordinary story, in both senses of that word: it is as remarkable as it is exceptional. I'm not sure whether it should be shared, as it is certain to give the wrong impression. But then, I think, it might be the exception that proves the rule. Well, be that as it may, I will tell it as I observed it, although, yes, at times I may fill in a few gaps from my imagination. Maybe, I don't know all the facts and all the motivations of the characters involved, but I am certain that there are lessons to be learned and there is much food for thought from what I do know.

It was 1978 when I joined the United Nations. In those days, no one had heard of a Code of Conduct, and standards of behaviour were implicit rather than documented. We were expected to do no harm, to behave with the highest of standards. When the wife of the head of office used the office car for personal shopping, or a staff member took stationery home for personal use, or a manager had a sexual relationship with one of his staff, we were neither shocked nor surprised. These things were not considered wayward. No one told us that they were.

We sort of knew where to draw the line though. Stealing money from the organisation, bribing government officials, accepting bribes (apart from smallish gifts), or exploiting refugees and the poor were probably beyond the pale, although I do recall cases where it was reported to have happened.

Anyway, I will tell my story, and you can form your own judgement as to the ethical standards of the characters involved.

Derailment

November 2017

It was not until later that I knew whether Gemma Soriano was deliberately poisoned or whether it was just a normal case of food poisoning. Travellers who stayed at the Hill Town Hotel in Addis Ababa often, it seemed, suffered from foodborne illness. The classic symptoms were evident: nausea, diarrhea, vomiting, and stomach cramps. Poisons, such as lead, arsenic and cyanide can bring on the same symptoms, I am told. I remember well how I suffered from food poisoning when I went on a mission to Addis in 1990. Surely the hygiene conditions would have improved since then, but who knows?

The Hill Town was the preferred hotel for visiting UN staff. It provided an attractive UN discount, and it was but a short walk to the UN compound and conference centre, known as Africa Hall. So, it was not a surprise that a reservation was made there for Gemma. She did not complain. It was a comfortable hotel and the cost of the room and board was well within the prevailing daily subsistence allowance for those on duty travel to Ethiopia. There would be some savings to be had from this mission, which was a monetary bonus not to be refused.

That being said, Gemma did not like travelling away from New York, even though it was very much part of her job description. "This position will require frequent travel," it said. When she applied for the position, she could have listened to the little voice at the back of her head which, for that reason, counselled against accepting it, but the lure of New York was just too great. One is never rational when applying for posts. The job description is read selectively and the proverbial greener grass over the fence erases most rationality.

Truth be known, her inspection mission to the Economic

Commission for Africa (ECA) in Addis was pretty much routine. Later in the year she would undertake a similar mission to Santiago, to the Economic Commission for Latin America. Nothing very particular about these missions and Gemma actually found them rather boring.

On her second working day in Addis, as she was eating breakfast in the hotel dining room, a young lady approached her.

"My name is Nyala Beyene. We were introduced briefly yesterday in the office. I am a finance assistant. May I talk to you when you have finished your breakfast?"

"Yes, of course. I do remember you. Why don't you join me and take a tea or coffee?"

"I would prefer not. May I talk to you with more privacy? I shall wait for you in the garden near the swimming pool if you don't mind. No hurry."

Gemma was intrigued, quickly completed her breakfast, and exited the French doors through the terrace to the pool area. She spotted Nyala lurking in the bushes adjacent to the pool.

"How can I help?"

"It may be nothing, but I have a sense, nothing I can pin down, that my boss, Thabisa Maseko, is doing something unprofessional, and possibly illegal. I am told that whistle-blowers can be protected from retribution. I am scared. I would not have said anything, but when I met you yesterday, I felt obliged to say something and I thought you might be sympathetic to my concerns. I do not want to lose my job, nor make any false accusations. Please, please, can you be very discreet if you choose to investigate?"

"Thank you, Nyala, for coming to see me. You did the right thing in doing so. Leave it to me. I will be very cautious and your name will not be mentioned."

They parted ways and Nyala left for work, troubled by what she had done. She had heard of cases where the organisation, while espousing zero tolerance on many matters of staff conduct, still preferred to sweep uncomfortable revelations under the rug. In addition, she reflected, her own conduct in the office was not without fault.

Gemma had a full agenda. Her standard inspection checklist was long and included amongst other things: reviewing recruitment procedures; checking compliance of the performance appraisal system; reviewing the ECA's role as lead UN Agency in Ethiopia and as the designated agency for staff safety and security; the efficiency of the shared UN premises in the vast UN compound; and while not undertaking a full audit, looking into matters of financial management. The last of these included an inspection of the implementation of UNSFIS. This gave her ample opportunity to talk to Thabisa and review the financial management system without raising any alarm bells.

For her part, Thabisa's radar was working overtime and anything out of the ordinary made her nervous. She was aware that Gemma's mission was routine, but she could not shake her apprehension. Indeed, she had reason to worry, but more about that later. I am jumping ahead of myself. I should relate this tawdry tale from the beginning.

Integrity

April 2015

As supply officer in a Country Office for several years, Peter has become very knowledgeable about import and export requirements, and the bureaucratic intricacies of trade in the region. In addition, his personal relationships with relevant government officials have been particularly useful on occasions when his agency had experienced humanitarian goods being delayed at the port customs facility.

Peter's wife, Kathy, has been interested in oriental carpets for many years and has a large collection herself. Recently she has begun purchasing a few carpets at the local bazaar and selling them to friends and relatives in her home country. She discovered there is a demand for the carpets and has decided to open a carpet exporting business. Peter's experience and knowledge turns out to be very useful to her, and he becomes directly involved with his wife's business and facilitates all the customs arrangements for the exportation of the carpets at favourable rates. From time to time, to help the process, he needs to "grease the palms" of the customs officials.

One day, Kathy invites Melinda to her house and shows her the carpets and mentions, in passing, the help that Peter is giving her. As a colleague and friend of Peter, Melinda would prefer to ignore what she has discovered, but as a staff member she knows that there may be a problem here and Peter's behaviour should be reported. What should Melinda do?

"Now, in your groups you have 30 minutes to look at this scenario and with reference to the UN Code of Conduct and the Standards of Conduct of International Civil Servants, identify which clauses might apply. Then, come up with recommendations on what course of action Melinda should take."

Akiko had done this exercise many times before. She had in her arsenal a whole range of scenarios and found that they generated a good deal of discussion and brought the Code of Conduct training alive. Hers was just one session in the broader middle management and leadership training held regularly by the College.

While the six groups of four participants from many different agencies in the United Nations System were getting down to their deliberations, Akiko looked out the window of the pavilion. She never tired of the view. The River Po was higher than normal, as the snows were melting on the Conca Cialancia Alps. That, combined with the spring rains, had swollen the river. Not as bad as the previous year when the river rose above its banks, the campus flooded, and the training nearly had to be aborted.

Akiko had been at the UN System Staff College for two years and loved training staff. Although she was not directly helping refugees, distributing food, building schools, combating child labour or working in the multifarious activities of the vast UN System, she deeply believed that staff training would have a positive impact on the behaviour of staff who attended these development programmes.

She was not so naïve to ignore the fact that staff considered training workshops as a perk. Who wouldn't like a few days in Turin and a break from the pressures of the office? They came from comfortable capital cities like Rome, Paris, Geneva but also from the deep field: Jigjiga, Kaga Bandoro, Muangdaw, Cúcuta and so many small towns of which most people had never heard, let alone expected to visit or live in their lifetimes. Many staff joked that they wanted a break from the hardship of headquarters offices such as New York, with its interminable meetings and pervasive office politics and to be transferred to the deep field, to the "coalface", where the real work is done.

But in both cases, a few days in Turin was most welcome, where the weather was fine and, in the College cafeteria, the cuisine Italian. What more needed to be said? Participating in a training workshop was considered a perk, even an acquired right. Attendance was eagerly sought and the subject of much jealousy when not shared equitably.

Akiko looked at her watch. "Ten minutes more," she announced. One group was clearly finished already. They thought they were efficient, but she knew it was probably because there was a dominant personality in the group who was certain of the answers, dictated his views (it usually was a "him"), and stifled any discussion. That was the kind of hubristic personality on whom leadership training was wasted.

The participants regrouped in plenary and Akiko, in her perfect script, a must for every good trainer, wrote the conclusions on the flip chart. *Conflict of interest; using office resources and time for private business; a family member benefiting from a staff member's position; engaging in unacceptable and possibly corrupt practices with local officials; potentially bringing the name of the United Nations into disrepute; inadequate disclosure of inappropriate activities; potential export of antique items and thus contravening local laws.* A nice list, Akiko thought. The message must have sunk in. It was a good scenario as Peter's activities breached so many standards.

"And what course of action would you take after hearing about this from Kathy?" Akiko asked. "Buy a few carpets," someone shouted. There was always a comedian in the group. Well once the group had offered some ideas, there was consensus that there was a case for dismissal or, at a minimum, a reprimand, a transfer to a different duty station, and a freeze on promotion for a period.

Of course, there was a heated debate about whether Melinda should "spill the beans" and tell the Head of Office or alternatively take Peter aside and give him a chance to redeem his ways and stop the practices. "No, that second option is complicit, and Melinda would be equally in breach of the Code of Conduct," someone said. Akiko had to agree with that stance, as the Secretary General had made it clear on so many occasions that there was zero tolerance when it came to matters of conduct. International civil servants were to adhere to the highest standards of behaviour. The wriggle room option did not exist.

"Time for lunch. We meet again at two for José's session on leadership and emotional intelligence. Bon appétit."

Serendipity

Four United Nations staff members and a chance encounter. It's the stuff of crime fiction, don't you think? What are the chances that these four would meet and hatch a plan that goes contrary to everything in which they once believed? They were not bad people. They did not even consider themselves criminals, although there was no doubt that is what they had become. None of them started out that way. At best, they all believed in the values and mission of the United Nations. At worst, and that can't really be faulted, they just found the work interesting, the salary and benefits rewarding, and the chance of travel satisfying. If you were to ask them, they would probably say that working for the United Nations was more noble than working for a tobacco company, an arms manufacturer or a petroleum company, but for some it was just a job.

Take Hamiz for example. One would assume that an Anti-Corruption Advisor was uncorruptible. Indeed, had you asked him what he thought of the core UN values of integrity and professionalism just two years ago, there is no doubt how he would have responded. He still believed in professionalism, even if it was now misdirected.

Alejandra was a technician. She never saw a refugee, an undernourished child or a trafficked woman in the course of her work. Alejandra interacted with a computer most of the time and met with her IT colleagues and discussed coding, programming and systems architecture. But that did not mean she did not have a conscience. Yes, she came from a wealthy family, but she did encounter 10-year-old boys and girls washing windscreens at traffic lights – she gave them a few pesos and felt redeemed – and bought a few *huaraches* with *frijoles* from the old lady outside her school, after her class – and believed she was sharing her income. Alejandra was a firm believer in "trickle down" economics.

And then there was Kyros, who was well suited in his communications role. He could sell anybody anything, usually with his own benefit in mind. He rarely did anything constructive, unless he had to. A minimalist, would be one way to describe his work ethic, but he fooled most of the people most of the time with his confident talk. Kyros had the ability to make the most mundane ideas seem sensible and cutting edge. He was the most likely to compromise any principles he may have had, were it to be to his personal benefit. His boss had a favourite expression: "If I could buy people for what they are worth, and sell them for what they think they are worth, I would be a rich man." It is possible that he was thinking of Kyros when he said that.

Thabisa, she knew about poverty. Growing up in Giyani in Northern Transvaal was not the most auspicious of beginnings. Giyani was not much changed since the apartheid days. It was miserable then and was a miserable place when Thabisa grew up. Good fortune, good luck or simply hard work helped Thabisa escape a life of poverty and eventually get a respectable position in finance at the United Nations. You can wonder, was it a knowledge of the inequity in life that justified a wavering of her moral conduct?

Anyway, here they were, four potential leaders in the UN – why else might they have been chosen to attend a leadership training workshop? – eating pasta and salad *al fresco* in the garden of the UN System Staff College outside the cafeteria.

Day three of the five-day training workshop. The conversation started off with the usual predictability. "Where are you stationed?" "Do you happen to know Fazli Farooqi? He works at UNIDO in Vienna." "How long have you worked for the UN?" "How were you recruited?"

Then, with equal predictability it turned to the training itself. "Is this your first training workshop with the UN?" "What do you think of the Staff College Campus?" "How were you selected for this training?" "What did you think of the last session?"

Thabisa: "I liked the exercise, it was fun."

Hamiz: "It was a bit obvious. I found it a waste of time."

Thabisa: "Well, I guess you would. You are an anti-corruption advisor. You work with these issues every day."

Alejandra: "Hamiz, was that a likely scenario?"

Hamiz: "I am sure that there are staff who would do that without thinking twice."

Alejandra: "I find that hard to believe. Staff working for the UN behaving corruptly?"

Kyros: "Alejandra, don't be so naïve. I'm sure it happens all the time."

Thabisa: "What would motivate people to do that?"

Hamiz: "So many reasons – envy, greed, inferiority complex, sense of invincibility, influence of others, sense of power ... the list goes on."

Alejandra: "Well at least now that we have had the training we are aware of what to avoid and how to behave."

Kyros: "I agree we know what is expected of us, but you should not kid yourself that a 40-minute exercise in a workshop is a guarantee of ethical behaviour."

They all sat in silence for a while. Food was over, food for thought not. It was just before two. Time to return to the classroom pavilion. Alejandra and Thabisa walked ahead. Hamiz and Kyros behind.

"I am convinced we could all succumb if the circumstances coalesced in such a way that temptation presented itself," Hamiz said.

"I think I agree," said Kyros. "Even I, at times, have been frustrated. I see staff promoted above me. I see others not performing."

"I guess for me, if, and I say if, I were to waver from the straight and narrow, it would be greed that would tempt me."

"That is a rather startling revelation, Hamiz. Don't you feel you get enough monetary benefits from the UN? You get a good salary, an education grant for the children, a paid trip home to see your family every two years, global health insurance. What more could you want?"

"It's not for me. I have a large family at home in Pakistan. Not just my wife and children, but brothers, sisters, my parents, aunts, uncles. They all see me as the success in the family and the bread winner for the clan. The pressure is immense."

"Do you really think if the situation arose, you could be corrupted?"

"I wish you would not use that word. 'Corrupted' sounds so despicable. But if you ask, could I be tempted, then I think I might. Indeed, I think everyone could."

"Do you really believe that? What about Alejandra and Thabisa? Could they be tempted to steal from the organisation? They are very different of course. Thabisa grew up in poverty and Alejandra in luxury. Do the rich desire more wealth or the poor desire the wealth of the rich? Greed versus envy. An interesting conundrum, don't you think?"

"I am prepared to bet that we could even convince Alejandra and Thabisa to behave corruptly."

"Is that a challenge?"

"Why not treat it as such? We need not follow through, but let's pursue that challenge."

Hamiz and Kyros caught up with Alejandra and Thabisa.

Hamiz said, "Thanks for your company at lunch. We enjoyed the conversation. Why don't we go out tonight together to a restaurant and continue? I will ask the receptionist for a restaurant recommendation. Shall we meet at seven at the reception?"

They readily agreed and entered the classroom, eager to become more emotionally intelligent.

Epicuriosity

At seven, as agreed, the four new friends met at the gates of the campus.

Hamiz said, "The man at the reception recommends we go to Piazza Vittorio Veneto. He claims that square is one of the most magnificent piazzas in all of Italy and we should not leave Turin without having seen it. He proposed a very simple pizzeria on the piazza, typical of the region; family owned and run. Apparently Torino pizzas are very special, although he said they have pasta and other dishes too. It's called Da Michele. Let's give it a try if you all agree."

They ordered a taxi which followed the river to the piazza. The receptionist was not wrong.

"Wow," Alejandra said, "this is grand and unusual."

Piazza Vittoria Veneto was not strictly speaking a square and not fully enclosed. It was an elongated U with the open side facing the river and the curve with its back to the city centre. An avenue ran through the centre of the piazza from the river to the town centre. If you looked across the Po, at the end of the Vittorio Emanuele I bridge, there stood the parish church of the Grand Mother of God. Do not imagine a small parish church. Imagine neo-classical grand, deserving of the Virgin Mary. A circular domed heavy construction was fronted with a façade of Roman columns, flanked by two statues on large plinths. It was not unlike a smaller version of the Pantheons in Paris or in Rome. Naturally in front of the columns was a grand statue of Vittorio Emanuele I himself, gazing towards Pizzeria Da Michele in the distance.

Piazza Vittoria Veneto was three times as long as it was wide. The five storey buildings abutting the piazza were impressive, to say the least, the ground level equivalent to two, maybe even three stories, and the facades comprised the arcades for which Turin was famous.

"It just occurred to me, that it was in Turin, and under

these arcades, that the famous car chase in the original *Italian Job* movie took place," Kyros commented.

The buildings on the left of the piazza were a mirror of those on the right, providing perfect symmetry. And, at the top left corner, under the arches was the modest Pizzeria Da Michele.

As the four approached, they saw a large outdoor seating area on the piazza. Inside there were two dining areas, one of which had about 10 classically set tables with white table-cloths looking very Italian. Along one side was a counter of white classic tiles, marble top and behind, a wood-fired pizza oven. A small separate wine bar and coffee servery was in the corner, dominated by the Rolls Royce, or, should one more appropriately say, Maserati, of espresso machines.

They were relatively early and the restaurant was not yet full. They chose to sit in the room with the bar and pizza oven as it provided a more authentic experience. The menu was extensive. A bottle of Borolo from Piemonte (Hamiz did drink alcohol) and sparkling water were ordered while they perused the menu.

Kyros, looking at the menu said, "Look what I see amongst the pizza options. I'll have this for sure. They have gorgonzola and pear pizza. Three nights ago, at the welcome cocktail party for the course, over the copious chunks of Parmesan and never-ending slices of Parma ham, I was talking to the director of the Staff College, Wolfgang Aldobrandeschi. No doubt you, as I, have been curious about the incongruity of his bilingual name. So, I asked him. He is Austrian as you know, and apparently the Aldobrandeschi family was a noble dynasty in the Duchy of Siena. In the 17th century a member of the family moved to Vienna and had a distinguished military career. The director told me that his great-grandfather, Rudolf Graf Aldobrandeschi degli Cabrini was chief of the Austro-Hungarian navy from 1904 to 1913. I didn't know that the Austro-Hungarian Empire had a navy, but he explained that, at that time, the Empire encompassed what is now Slovenia and Croatia so operated out of the Adriatic. Apparently, the Graf was responsible for the modernisation of the Austrian naval fleet."

As was often the case, Kyros was rambling. He loved talking and showing off his knowledge and, above all, the fact that he had had a conversation with the director. Kyros liked to drop names.

"Yes, yes, all very interesting, Kyros, but what about the pizza?" Thabisa was not being aggressive, it was not in her nature, but she was curious and hungry.

"Ah, indeed. The director, while quintessentially Austrian, is very much an Italophile. He speaks Italian fluently and is intimately familiar with local customs. I asked him what I should eat while here, what is typical of the region. He mentioned a few dishes, but said that at the top of his personal list is the gorgonzola and pear pizza. He said that there is an old Italian proverb:

Al contadino non far sapere,

quanto è buono il formaggio con le pere.

Which translated means: "Do not let the farmer know how good cheese is with pears." I asked him how this proverb is to be interpreted, apart from the obvious that cheese and pear go well together. He said that the expression is typically used when we have information we don't want to reveal." Kyros looked at Hamiz and smiled. "I like the expression and now I will see whether I like the pizza."

The waiter arrived and recommended the pizza but also said that they had a selection of excellent pastas. He had with him a plate with a sample of five different uncooked pastas.

"This is tagliatelle, it comes with a wild boar ragu; this is pappardelle and comes with our special mixed seafood sauce with black pepper; this one is agnolotti, which is filled with courgette and comes with a wild mushroom cream sauce; this is orecchiette, because the pasta looks like little ears, and it is served with anchovy and garlic; and finally this pasta is called caserecce and has a spicy arrabiata sauce with tomatoes and chilis from our own garden."

"It's just too much. It's impossible to make a choice."

The waiter smiled. It was a smile he had perfected when confronted with the reaction that most foreign guests gave when faced with too much choice. The locals were simple eaters. They cherished a good pizza margarita, or if they took pasta, they would not have craved for more than a very basic cream sauce, ragu or tomato sugo, as long as, of course, the pasta was fresh and cooked to perfection. But tourists liked complexity in their food. If the pizza had six or more ingredients, that was tantalising. A true Italian would be satisfied with just one or two toppings.

"Maybe what I can propose," the waiter went on, "is that you try them all. Let me serve you a tasting of all five. They will be small helpings. And then you can follow up with a pizza of your choice. Our pizzas are small, just the size of a soup plate. You may even have room for panna cotta or tiramisu. How does that sound?"

They readily agreed. They anticipated a plate each with five pastas, but, oh no. A true Italian would never mix the flavours. God forbid that the sauces may touch! So, one by one, a large white porcelain plate was served to each diner with a tiny taste to titillate: three agnolotti, six orecchiette, seven caserecce and so on. Heaven. There followed the pizza, which, after the eloquent commendation from Kyros, could be no other than gorgonzola with pear – the gorgonzola melted, the thinly sliced pear momentarily singed and the rucola fresh. Over a second bottle of Borolo, they were full of praise.

The conversation was friendly and bonding took place. Aspects of their personal lives shared, work concerns aired, and experiences compared.

Kyros looked at Hamiz. Hamiz looked at Kyros. Kyros, not surprisingly, bit the bullet and began. "Hamiz and I were reflecting after lunch about our discussion. We would like to raise a hypothetical. We admitted to each other that under the right circumstances we might succumb to temptation and do something unethical, me out of envy and a sense that I have not been valued by the organisation, and Hamiz – if you permit me to share Hamiz – for financial gain."

Hamiz blushed and interrupted, "We are not saying we will do it, just imagining under what circumstances, hypothetical of course, we might. When would opportunity and motive coalesce, we wonder?"

There was some silence. Had Kyros and Hamiz gone too far? Alejandra looked at Thabisa, who shrugged her shoulders with that "don't look at me" look.

Realising she should not embarrass Kyros and Hamiz, and choosing to break a certainly awkward silence, Alejandra said, "Okay, hypothetically of course, what kind of ideas could we come up with?"

Kyros: "It would need to be something where the rewards are worth the risks."

Alejandra: "That would suggest something financial."

Hamiz: "Where is the most money in the system?"

Kyros: "I suspect with the big operational agencies like UNDP, UNICEF and UNHCR."

Thabisa: "Actually, with UNSFIS, the new integrated financial management scheme, all the funds from most agencies are consolidated in one place. Of course, the funds are in different banks in many different countries, but the management and control of these funds is centralised."

Alejandra: "Any idea how much we are talking about?"

Thabisa: "Well, let's just take the three you mentioned Kyros. UNDP, UNICEF and UNHCR all have regular budgets and special operations and it's hard at any time to measure the magnitude of their budgets, income and expenditure, but more or less all three have annual budgets of just over five billion dollars. Peacekeeping operations are about the same.

And that's just the tip of the iceberg really. But there is no way to embezzle any large amounts without it being noticed."

Alejandra: "How many transactions would be processed through the system in any day?"

Thabisa: "Impossible to say off-hand, but several thousand probably."

Alejandra: "Hypothetically, of course, if one siphoned off just one cent per transaction, that might amount to about one hundred thousand dollars a month."

Thabisa: "Quite possibly."

Kyros and Hamiz looked at each other with shared amazement about the (hypothetical) enthusiasm and reasoning of Alejandra and Thabisa.

They were all silent for a while. Each was having a bout of self-reflection.

Is this discussion really happening?

Is this the real me?

What are the others thinking?

This will never happen, will it?

Shouldn't I suggest we stop this discussion before it gets out of hand?

No one said, "I think we should stop this discussion. I think it's going too far." For some reason they all had a sense of excitement, an adrenaline rush, and they sensed it not only in themselves but in the others.

They were interrupted by the waiter. "Anyone care for dessert, coffee or a *digestivo*?" Dessert seemed out of the question after that meal and they reluctantly declined, so the waiter proposed espresso and a limoncello or a good grappa del Piemonte. "I can recommend an amber muscatel grappa. It's not too strong, slightly sweeter than others, and an excellent example of what the local region has to offer." The waiter was a salesman as well as very Italian – or is that tautology?

They made their choices. Decaffeinated espresso would

not be efficacious as, after the foregoing discussion, easily falling asleep would be out of the question in any case.

The four agreed that the (hypothetical) discussion should be continued. They probably needed to be discreet, so they arranged to have lunch separately the next day, but after lunch go for a walk along the river before the afternoon classes. The conspiratorial feel to that arrangement was not lost on any of them.

It was such a lovely evening they decided to walk some of the way back to the Staff College campus. They traversed the piazza, walked along the Corso Cairoli beside the river and through the Parco del Valentino, after which they caught a taxi back to the campus. The only conversation on the way to the college residence was about the food.

Aspiration

I guess it's time I told you about our four would-be criminals. As I said, they did not start out in life with any ill intent. Indeed, their convergent paths into the United Nations, while their starting points dissimilar, were not atypical of so many of their colleagues.

Let's start with Alejandra Castillo Rivera, who was known fondly by her parents and others as Ale. When she turned 16 years old, and she felt that she was now a mature young lady, she rejected the nickname and insisted that her friends, but not her parents for whom the adjustment may have been too abrupt, call her Alejandra. So out of respect, I shall do the same.

Alejandra was born into privilege, in a spacious eight-bedroom house in Lomas de Chapultepec, Mexico City. The house was surrounded by a high wall with state-of-the-art security. Her parents believed it important that she receive a bilingual education, so Alejandra went, as did her younger sister, to the prestigious British American School. She did not take the school bus, but was driven by Manuel, the chauffeur, not so much for convenience but for her own security. Eduardo Castillo was in the property and construction business, although he never talked about his work with his children and curiously, when he talked about his work to Christina, his wife, it was always in hushed tones. Alejandra was conditioned from an early age not to ask.

Alejandra was a most attractive young woman. For Mexican standards she had fair skin, deep blue eyes and to accentuate the contrast, jet-black hair, which she let fall below her shoulders. She was rather tall and walked and spoke with confidence. She exuded charm.

After completing her secondary school studies, Alejandra chose to leave Mexico City, and took a three-year bachelor's course in information technology at the Tecnológico de

Monterrey, where she graduated with honours. Next stop, a masters at the Massachusetts Institute of Technology. All this, a typical educational trajectory, facilitated by privilege and wealth.

At the annual MIT jobs fair, with little idea what to do next, she attended an interview with an officer from the Office of Human Resources Management of the United Nations. She was encouraged to apply for IT positions, one in New York and one in Geneva. She was, not unhappily, accepted to the latter and at the age of 25 joined the United Nations International Computing Centre, the UNICC.

Alejandra loved Geneva – its cleanliness, international character, the lake and its surroundings. It was a pleasant change from Mexico City and even Monterrey. What made it more special was that it was here that she fell in love. She was already fluent in Spanish and English, but felt that living in Geneva, she should learn French, even though the *lingua franca* (excuse the non-pun) in the office was English. Three mornings a week, before going to the office, Alejandra took lessons at the UN language school at the main UN building, the Palais des Nations. It was here on the first day of class, that she met Gabriel, a Peruvian who was working, essentially freelance, for various news agencies and dailies in Latin America, including the Adina news agency and La República in Peru, El Mercurio in Chile and a few others which would often run his stories. Actually, Gabriel saw himself as a budding writer of fiction novels, but was not yet published and needed to make a living as a journalist.

Alejandra and Gabriel dated for a while, actually a very short while, and moved into an apartment together in Grand-Saconnex, equidistant between the offices assigned to the accredited journalists in the Palais des Nations and the UNICC situated near Cointrin airport. They married in a registry office in Geneva, promising their respective parents that they would have a church wedding in Mexico or Peru at a later date.

Alejandra could not complain about her career path. She started at the entry level grade as an associate IT officer in the Platform Services Section, supporting the implementation of an Oracle Enterprise Resource Planning platform at one of the smaller UN Agencies based in Geneva. She quickly became an expert in the financials software and when a position at a higher grade arose three years later, she applied and was promoted to IT officer, taking on more independent responsibilities. Alejandra was clearly a highflyer and her selection to attend the leadership training in Turin was not a surprise.

If Alejandra was a highflyer, Kyros Balaskas grovelled close to the ground. He was born in Athens and after graduating from the Department of Communications and Mass Media of the Kapodistrian University, he worked for five years as a communications and public relations officer at a large Greek shipping enterprise. In 2006, Kyros applied for a local position with the small office of the United Nations High Commissioner for Refugees in Athens as public information officer. This was a two-year contract, and it can be assumed that it was not renewed for performance reasons, although Kyros always claimed that it was due to funding constraints.

Since the writing was "on the wall", Kyros applied widely in the UN system for other posts and, probably due to his excellent communication and interview skills (forgive me, but here you should read: ability to bullshit), he was appointed to a mid-level position at the International Telecommunications Union (ITU) in Geneva.

By this time Kyros was divorced and he went to Geneva alone. He found a nice semi-detached townhouse in the dormitory village of Versonnex, across the border in France and became one of the many *frontaliers,* commuting by car each day the few kilometres to Geneva. His title was Senior Communications Officer and, although he performed a range of functions working with the telecommunications ministries of member states on communications systems, much of the work was routine. He applied often for higher positions at the Chief of Section level, but was unsuccessful. After a while he noticed that those appointed to Chiefs of Sections were more junior than him.

He was now 45 years old and his frustration grew. He was convinced that he was effective. His supervisors were convinced he was lazy and did not have the necessary management competencies nor the potential for advancement. There were no real grounds for dismissal, so he was "parked" where he could do minimal harm. He was sent to Turin for the leadership training because he complained frequently to his supervisor that he was never selected for training workshops. He was selected this time because his boss could no longer face his constant moaning.

As you have already learned, Thabisa Maseko is one of that rare breed that escaped poverty and ended up at the UN. There are many routes to becoming an international staff member, the most common being to get a university degree, get some years of appropriate work experience under your belt and then apply for a vacancy that suits your qualifications. When doing so, most applicants believe that they are so well suited to the advertised job, that their selection is a shoo-in. Of course, so do the other one thousand applicants for the same job. After applying, all they think about is that dream job and each morning open their email expecting the call for an interview and each morning they are disappointed. This can go on for months. The chances are that they will never get the call, frustration and disbelief increasing. Language skills, nationality and gender might drop you off the short list even before skills and work experience are considered. It's the lack of feedback that gets to them. If only they were aware that several thousand applicants were in the same boat.

There is another route, the one that Kyros took. Getting a job at a local UN field office and getting some UN experience under your belt and then trying to "go international". Kyros got a professional job in Greece, but all Thabisa could strive for was a local general service position, that is a secretarial, clerical or other locally recruited support job.

Thabisa left Giyani, after being awarded the town's only education scholarship, to go to the Capricorn High School in Pietersburg, a year before the town, in 2005, changed its name to Polokwane. Thabisa was accommodated at the school's Southveld Hostel for girls, donned her rather snazzy school uniform (white blouse, blue and purple striped tie, blue blazer and matching skirt and a fetching cream boater), and lived the school motto *"Not just a school, but a way of life"*. She loved the school and performed well. She excelled in mathematics and left the highschool with another scholarship to the University of the Witwatersrand in Johannesburg, where she was accommodated in one of the campus residences. Thabisa graduated with a degree in accounting, responded to an advertisement at the United Nations Development Programme (UNDP) in Pretoria, and facilitated by her engaging smile, youthful confidence, and high passing grades, was offered a job as a finance assistant.

From the outset Thabisa had higher aspirations and was not satisfied with a support role. She strived for more responsibility and when after three years a professional post of Associate Finance Officer became available, she was an obvious choice for the position. After six years at UNDP, she applied for a Finance Officer post in Addis Ababa at the UN

Economic Commission for Africa and was now happily ensconced as an international staff member with a promising future.

Every morning, as she walked from her apartment in nearby Kazanchis to her office on the fifth floor of the ECA building, Thabisa reflected on her good fortune. She had been blessed with a good education and a well-paying job. But there was still something missing. Was it loneliness or was it boredom with the routine? What good is life if there is no spark of excitement?

Hamiz Baig was born in Lahore. His family was not rich, nor were they poor. His father was a civil servant in the Punjab provincial government and his mother a primary school teacher. Theirs was an arranged marriage and it was assumed that their two daughters and two sons would also have arranged marriages.

Hamiz grew up in a home in which education was valued. His parents did not, as was the case in many households, consider that their daughters' place was in the home and all four children were encouraged to go to the University of Lahore.

Hamiz entered the College of Law at the university and specialised in criminology. Like his siblings he lived at home and once he secured his first job and was economically self-sufficient, he was married to the daughter of a one of his father's colleagues, whom Hamiz had met for the first time not long before their wedding. The future bride and groom had little say in the matter, but they did have much in common, and as far as arranged marriages were concerned they were sure they could grow to love each other.

They set up house in Islamabad, where Hamiz had secured a good position in the National Accountability Bureau (NAB), which was charged with reducing corruption in all sectors of Pakistani society. This was a major undertaking and Hamiz soon learned that the issues with which he dealt were not black and white. He was encouraged quite frequently to arrange plea bargains and out-of-court settlements as this was the path of least inconvenience. Justice was seen to be done, but the impact on the prevalence of corruption was not as should have been expected. Then there were the instances where opponents of the government were arrested and held on trumped up charges. The NAB was at times a blunt and misguided weapon.

Hamiz accepted this as "just the way things are done" and took his salary, did what was expected of him to the best of his ability and fathered three children in quick succession. His wife gave up her part-time job and became a full-time mother and Hamiz, who tended to envy the riches of others (and he crossed paths with many in his line of work), was not fully satisfied with his lot.

In the course of his work, he was asked to liaise with a visiting official from the UN Office on Drugs and Crime from Vienna. UNODC worked frequently with member states on capacity building. Hamiz assisted the official with his fact finding and arranging his meetings. In other words, he was a baby-sitter, but he did well and left a good impression. A few weeks later he was called into his boss's office and asked if he would like a secondment to UNODC in Vienna. This, as they say, was a "no brainer", and was the answer to his financial aspirations. The pay was much better and there was a health care scheme and education grants for the children.

He and his wife agreed (well, she complied, might be a better choice of words) that he would go alone to Vienna and, for the sake of their "children's stability", his wife and children would remain in Pakistan.

The secondment was extended twice and when Hamiz was appointed to the position of Global Anti-corruption Advisor, the very position that his mentor held when he visited Pakistan, it was decided to convert the secondment into a formal recruitment.

Hamiz was given a paid visit on Home Leave once every two years as part of his contract. Occasionally, if he went on mission to South Asia, he would detour for a few days to see his family. His family never visited Vienna. Hamiz was able to save half of his salary, which he sent to his wife. As he travelled quite often, the balance from the daily subsistence allowance, after paying for food and hotels, was an added income. Life was good, particularly since Hamiz was not averse to engaging in personal relationships with female colleagues.

Integration

As you may have noticed already, although I have tried to avoid them as much as possible so as not to confuse you, dear reader, the United Nations is acronym-paradise.

When new systems are introduced, the choice of acronym might be the subject of a special committee meeting. Consensus is important. The acronym must be manageable, it must have a ring, and ideally should be pronounceable. I am not sure who came up with UNSFIS, but it does have a kind of ring to it, and, unless one has a lisp, it is pronounceable.

Some years ago, most UN agencies decided to introduce Enterprise Resource Planning (ERP) systems, usually the finance and the human resources modules. Tenders were issued and Oracle, SAP and PeopleSoft and others competed for the lucrative UN business. There would certainly have been logic in all UN agencies selecting one integrated system, but that level of harmonisation was not to be.

Then there were the big debates about "off-the-shelf" or customisation. The established UN systems and processes did not fit easily into the off-the-shelf products so rather than adapt the systems to the ERP product, which most experts recommended, the ERP was adapted to the existing systems, which was generally not a good idea, for reasons which I need not bore you with here.

There were, however, some instances where UN agencies, which did talk to each other and plan together under an array of committee structures, did decide to harmonise systems, and the United Nations System Financial Integrated Scheme (UNSFIS) was born. It was a massive undertaking to integrate and adapt each agency's ERP into a global ERP. Cross-agency planning committees and inter-agency implementation committees were established. They met in New York, Geneva and Vienna. There were meetings of policy makers, resource and funding meetings with member states and key donors, and meetings of technicians. They dealt with the IT systems, cyber security, finance processes, deployment to remote offices, hardware requirements, standardisation and so many more issues. The best minds in all agencies were seconded full-time or part-time to the planning and implementation structures. The travel budget for attendance at these committee meetings increased as did consultant fees, but the objective was to achieve huge economies of scale, savings, and enhanced financial management and reporting across the UN System.

Just to give you an idea of the type of discussion:

"I don't think it makes sense to call it the United Nations System Financial Information System, We cannot have two 'systems' in the same acronym."

"We could drop the first 'system' and just call it the United Nations Financial Information System."

"Then the acronym, UNFIS, would be as easily pronounce-able."

"It sounds okay to me."

"Yes, but the notion of a UN System is important to the concept."

"Why don't we change the second 'system' to 'scheme', and then we keep the same acronym."

"Yep, that could work."

"My problem is with the 'I'. I think it's more than an information system, I mean scheme. I think the notion of integrated is important."

Well, you get the idea. This discussion lasted a good few hours and was finally resolved to the satisfaction of most but not all. In the end, it probably did not matter as the acronym became a word in itself and the components were lost in time.

Many meetings had greater relevancy, but decision making by committee, and all that that entailed, was the norm. Eventually the structure, or system, or was it scheme, evolved, expanded and emerged.

Some headquarters offices and some field offices were

selected as pilot countries and Addis Ababa was one of them. The UN has five regional economic commissions – in Africa, Asia Pacific, Latin America, Europe and the Middle East. The Economic Commission for Africa is situated in Addis Ababa and is housed in an impressive multistorey office complex attached to an equally grand conference centre, in what is known as the ECA compound. It houses the ECA as well as most of the offices of the other UN agencies in Addis.

As I have already indicated, Thabisa worked as Finance Officer at the ECA and, as such, was intimately involved in the pilot for the implementation of UNSFIS. She had been doing the work for three years and was thoroughly relieved that the pilot stage was over and roll-out was about to begin. Thabisa implemented the UNSFIS pilot at the ECA and with other participating agencies in Addis. There were frequent visits of IT staff from the International Computing Centre in Geneva, finance officers from the Department of Finance at the UN Secretariat in New York, and systems integrators from one of the big five consulting companies from London.

Thabisa was exhausted with the long hours involved, but nevertheless proud of what she had achieved, although she felt neither the ECA Director of Administration nor the ECA Executive Secretary recognised the effort she had exerted on the project, and with considerable success. Even her supervisor, the Chief of Finance, who should have known better, only gave her mediocre recognition in the last annual performance appraisal review. Thabisa was somewhat exploited and overworked, as she was expected to perform her normal finance functions as well as implement the UNSFIS pilot.

What she did enjoy was the opportunity to train staff in the use of the system. On her last mission to Geneva, for training in the system, she also attended a three-day training of trainers' workshop. Thabisa discovered that she had an aptitude for training and was told that she was engaging and motivating. It was the closest she could come to acting, which she would find a challenge, given her introverted nature. Now that the UNSFIS pilot was coming to an end, Thabisa became involved in training staff from all field offices in East and Central Africa in UNSFIS, who came to Addis for training.

The initial training phase was to last just one year and it was towards the end of this phase that Thabisa was sent to Turin for the leadership training.

Consummation

It's strange how certain things have their own momentum. They say a rolling stone gathers no moss, but we cannot say the same for a snowball. It transpired that the evolving discussion amongst what, for convenience's sake, I shall henceforth call "The Four", was less like the stone than the snowball, which, as it rolled, grew larger.

There came a point when there was no turning back. That point had not yet been reached, but, to mix metaphors, the seed was sown.

The Po was a sizable river at any time, and, as it flowed through Turin, it was an attractive river. This was particularly true adjacent to the UN System Staff College. The pavilions, which were constructed in 1961 for the Turin World Fair, were handed over to the International Labour Organisation as a training centre after the fair came to an end. The ILO, in turn, rented out one pavilion to the Staff College and made available classroom space for courses for UN staff. The campus had its own, perfectly adequate, accommodation for trainees. It was a pleasant environment for study, and, it would seem, for hatching conspiracies.

The river was flanked by pathways for walking and cycling. Willows lined the route, which was conducive for after-lunch strolling. The Four, that sunny Wednesday after-noon in early April, were walking together, after lunch, down river. Beside the river, where the path widened, they stopped, away from the walkers and the cyclists, sat on the bank and looked out across the river.

Alejandra: "Well, this is rather awkward. I feel like I am having a secret affair. I did not sleep at all last night. I am not sure whether it was from guilt or excitement."

33

Hamiz: "Me too. Let's set aside the guilt and concentrate on the excitement. If we were to siphon off funds, what resources would we need to manage that? For my part, I have a pretty good understanding of the pitfalls and the mistakes that corrupt officials tend to make. I need not relate them all now, but often it is a result of insecure communications – electronic surveillance, journalists posing as collaborators with hidden cameras, undercover police – or often it is because they do not want to share the spoils with co-conspirators or others who tweak to their schemes."

Kyros: "On communications' security, I am sure I can come up with a secure network. Video conferencing such as Zoom, most instant messaging systems and social media platforms can't be trusted for full security. Some boast end to end encryption, but even that can be suspect at times. I think I could establish a sufficiently secure system for our purposes."

Thabisa: "You guys will not get anywhere without me. UNSFIS is a complicated monster. Its architecture, connecting all the regional nodes so that they talk to each other, is unfathomable. Where simplicity would have sufficed, complexity is the norm. There is no doubt that an off-the-shelf financial package would have done the trick, but like the proverbial camel, this was not designed by one committee but many committees. This one has no resemblance to a camel at all. This animal is a creature worthy of science fiction. That being said, if anyone knows the system's functionality, look no further."

Alejandra: "That complexity might work in our favour. I am quite familiar with ERP systems, well, the vanilla versions anyway, but I am sure UNSFIS sufficiently mirrors the standard functionality. I assume all the data sits in the cloud. We just need to sort out two things. First where to access the system without being detected – directly to the cloud or through one of the terrestrial nodes. Second, at what stage in

34

the financials chain to intervene. For example, at the income stage, the payables or even the investments."

Kyros: "Look at the time. It's quarter to two already. We are supposed to be outside the classroom pavilion in 15 minutes for the group photograph. Can't be late for that. I heard someone say once, 'It's not what you learn, but how you look in the group photo that counts.' And if this plan comes to fruition, that photo will have a significance that is priceless, so to speak." Kyros was pleased with his little pun and smiled.

Hamiz: "Aren't we going too far? Isn't this getting out of hand? I get a sense we have an agreement here to proceed."

The Four turned to look each other in the eyes. They sensed agreement. Alejandra felt like a group hug might be in order, but the bonding had not yet progressed to that stage. Thabisa normally found it difficult to maintain eye contact – it was not in her nature – but to her own surprise she did.

Kyros: "Do we have agreement that we proceed, at least through the feasibility stage? If so, I shall work on a secure communication platform for the four of us. Even though Alejandra and I are both in Geneva, I believe that after this training we should not meet. All communication should be via the channel I set up. Agreed?"

The Four nodded in agreement and hurried back to the campus for the group photo. For the remaining two days of the training, they made every effort to sit apart, but at times there was fleeting mischievous eye contact across the training room.

Trust

Kyros, Alejandra, and three other Geneva-based staff who attended the Turin workshop, touched down at Cointrin Airport in Geneva. On the flight, Alejandra sat next to a child labour specialist from the International Labour Organisation, who was working on combating the exploitation of children by multinational clothing companies in countries such as Bangladesh, China, Turkey and Morocco. The companies either denied it or found some justification for the practice. It was an interesting conversation.

Alejandra wondered what was more despicable – exploitation by large enterprises or embezzlement by individuals. Was there a qualitative or simply a quantitative difference? Can the criminal acts of governments and enterprises excuse or justify the criminal acts of individuals? Of course, these were rhetorical questions, and she instinctively knew the answer. However, it seemed to her that one could justify all actions, if inclined to do so.

Alejandra looked out the window. The plane was reducing altitude and there was a magnificent view of Mont Blanc, still gleaming pure white as the sun reflected off the snow. They passed the Salève mountain, the snow there now completely melted. Below she spotted paragliders hovering beside the monolith. The week before someone had died as he jumped off the cliff and could not control the glider, or something malfunctioned or maybe he just decided to end his life. *Why do people stand on a cliff or a balcony and think about jumping, but don't? Why do people hold a kitchen knife and think about stabbing but don't? What is it in human nature that stops us doing harm to ourselves or others? Is it self-preservation or a behavioural code? What is the tipping point, the trigger, the fine line between good and evil?* Alejandra was bounced out of her thoughts as the wheels hit the tarmac and she was brought back to earth.

The newly trained leaders retrieved their suitcases; Alejandra took a bus the few stops to her home in Grand-Saconnex, and Kyros retrieved his car from the long-term parking and crossed the border into France under the airport runway and drove to his home in Versonnex. It was only a 10-minute drive.

Gabriel was pleased to see Alejandra home again and Alejandra found herself describing the training in detail to Gabriel. She realised that she was probably talking too much. It was clearly a nervous reaction to what she did not share with him. But he listened patiently to her description of the games they played to demonstrate teamwork, conflict resolution, negotiation skills and managing under-performance. Gabriel asked her if there was anything serious about the training. "Of course there was. The lessons learned from the games were what counted. And the food was amazing."

"Well, I hope there will be a good return-on-investment from your leadership training."

"Oh, I am pretty sure there will be," she said and hoped that her internal smile was not evident on the outside.

The International Telecommunications Union (ITU) is in the heart of the international organisations' district of Geneva. It stands near WIPO, UNOG, UNHCR, WTO, WMO, UNICEF, ILO, WHO, IOM and a range of other acronyms. It was founded in Paris in 1865, long before the United Nations, and had been part of the UN family since 1947. Kyros had an office to himself on the seventh floor of the ITU tower block, a privileged situation, not because of his status, but because of the view.

To the right he could see the grand approach to the Palais des Nations, the office of the United Nations in Geneva, the arcade of flags impressive in the spring breeze. Beyond the

World Intellectual Property Organisation, its concave glass façade shining like a parabolic reflector, Kyros had a good view of the Jura mountains in the distance. He never tired of the view.

Kyros started this Monday morning, as he did every morning, by taking a coffee and croissant in the 11th floor coffee shop. He was joined, as was often the case at morning coffee time, by Vasiliki, a Greek colleague, and also a creature of habit, who worked in the Telecommunications Standardisation Division. Naturally she asked Kyros about the training. Not missing an opportunity to wax lyrical about anything in which he was involved, Kyros was effusive about the importance and impact of the training.

"Do you really think that a five-day training can make one a better manager and leader?" Vasiliki asked.

"Absolutely. Not only were the sessions and trainers excellent, but I was in the company of the best and brightest in the UN system. I am convinced that the time I spent in Turin will be transformative to my situation."

Vasiliki wondered why she put up with Kyros. If she were to reflect, it was because she did not like to sit alone in the cafeteria, and she was not fully aware that her good reputation may be tarnished by association.

Kyros, adequately caffeinated, returned to his office and skimmed his emails to see if there was anything new. He did not expect much, as he was in the habit, like all his colleagues, of reviewing his inbox every evening, even during the weekend. He opened the calendar app on his phone, although to do so was redundant, as he knew he only had one meeting. The meeting was to start at ten and finish at six, with coffee and lunch breaks of course. It reminded him of that worn out joke: "I only eat one meal a day, I start in the morning when I wake and finish when I go to bed."

Kyros had been appointed as rapporteur for the session and was expected to make a summary of the discussions. This was high pressure work, as the notes were required very speedily. Sometimes he had to work through lunch to ensure the notes were ready for the afternoon session, but this was just a one-day meeting so the notes could be distributed after the meeting was over.

It was a working group meeting on the Financial Inclusion Global Initiative which was looking at ways to make banking more accessible, through digital banking, to those without access to a physical banking establishment. The ITU had brought together a range of government and private sector actors to establish common standards. Today's meeting was to discuss the specific issue of developing trust in digital financial services.

Just before ten, Kyros took the lift down to one of the conference rooms in the basement and took a seat at the front of the room next to the chair of the meeting, a representative from a global financial services company. The ITU project lead sat on the other side of the chairperson. The Spanish, French and English interpreters were already in their booths and the delegates were beginning to arrive.

All delegates reconfirmed the importance of trust and discussed issues such as cyber security, encryption standards, password protection and so on, as means to maintain customer trust. Kyros needed to concentrate, but from time to time his mind wandered back to his code of conduct training and Turin. Trust: he recalled Akiko's words, "It's easy to lose and very hard to regain." Indeed.

During the breaks, delegates retired to the hallway where coffee and cookies were available on a silver-metal tea trolley. At afternoon coffee time, Kyros grabbed a coffee and went outside to get some fresh air. He needed to breathe, to have a break from the rather heavy deliberations and the stuffy meeting room.

Trust. *Can I trust Alejandra, Thabisa and Hamiz?* he thought. *Can they trust me? Would I trust me? If we do*

39

proceed with this plan, we are, after all, by definition, un-trustworthy, are we not? This is indeed a dilemma. There must be a name for it? Kyros thought back to the exercise they all did in Turin to practise trust, collaboration and negotiation skills. The idea was to maximise your team's points: you could gain more points by double-crossing the other team, but if both teams attempted a double-cross, neither would get any points. Points are only maximised by sticking to negotiated agreements and for both teams to collaborate. *"Prisoner's Dilemma", that's what it was called. What stance did Alejandra, Thabisa and Hamiz take during the game? Did they choose to compete or collaborate? I can't remember. I know at times I was aggressive and proposed we renege on the agreement we negotiated with the other team. Someone in the group had the audacity to suggest that my masculinity was being exposed. I remember that, and it shocked me. I do recall the outcome though, we all competed, and we all lost, to the joy of the training facilitator who thus managed well to convey the learning points.*

Kyros returned to the meeting room, deep in thought, and found it hard to concentrate for the remainder of the afternoon. There were niggling thoughts, vague impressions, hovering at the back of his mind, the kind of thoughts that were not well defined, they lingered there and never seemed to reach that part of the brain where you can make sense out of them, let alone deal with them.

He brushed his thoughts aside and recalled that he had been assigned homework – to come up with the secure communications system that the Four could use for their "project".

He was too tired to write up the minutes that evening and also too tired to cook. On the way home, just after crossing the border, Kyros stopped at the Lebanese shop and picked up some mezze – falafel, hummus, baba ghanoush and pita bread. It was his standard go-to takeaway when he was too lazy to cook. He sat at his kitchen table and started to think about how best the Four could communicate.

He immediately ruled out the most common conferencing, messaging and social networking options, but was aware of an obscure chat facility developed by the offshoot of an Israeli company which had once upon a time in 1996, (wow that is a prehistoric era in technology time) developed ICQ, one of the first instant messaging systems. A couple of the original developers and a few recent "graduates" of the Israeli Defence Forces had worked on a system that was designed for spies, not supposedly available on the market, but a version had been leaked and was available through the dark web. Only the limited user product was retrievable. It had been shared as a "sand-box", a test prototype, as a kind of "let's see how this performs" version. The version that was eventually re-leased was for local area and wide area networks and cost an amount that only governments (and, not a small number of non-state actors) could afford.

Kyros knew that this system was not supported by the developer in any way and was a kind of relic, long forgotten, but for four people to communicate securely and remotely it would suffice. They needed little functionality although simultaneous audio, but not video which could be more easily hacked, was possible. What was essential though was that they needed to hide their IP addresses, so he figured out a complicated routing through five virtual private networks, with a system by which the VPN locations changed randomly. On top of that there was encryption. The program could be installed on fixed desktops, laptops and mobile devices. All messages were deleted and all trace removed automatically after the message was opened and marked as read. After 12 hours messages were automatically deleted. Messages could be sent to all the other three or could be a private dialogue between any two or three of the Four.

It did not take long to configure and by two in the morning

he had sent an email to Alejandra, Thabisa and Hamiz with a link to a downloadable application, instructions for setting passwords and an instruction to delete the email once the app was downloaded.

Validation

Kyros: Hello all. I am pretty sure I have set this chat room up as expected. I believe it's secure. Looking forward to collaborating with you.

Alejandra: Buenos días. Well received. Yep, also ready to get started. All good.

Hamiz: Thanks, Kyros. Very efficient. I guess we need to establish work plan. Since Thabisa is familiar with the UNSFIS functionality, I guess you, Thabisa, could work with Alejandra to figure out the way to hack the code to siphon the funds.

Alejandra: Sounds good to me. Will do.

Thabisa: Nice to chat. Give us a few days and we will come back with a proposal.

So, Thabisa spent much of the next few days reflecting on the possibilities. UNSFIS comprised several modules: accounting; revenue management and receivables; payables and cash flow forecasting; asset management and control; exchange rate management; and diagnostics and reporting. In the background there was a complicated exchange rate database applying the unique UN exchange rate, which not only calculated average exchange rates, but recorded exchange rate gains and losses. There was the most detailed, some would say unnecessarily detailed, coding for expenditure items. Did it really matter if, in the big scheme of things, the system could tell you at a glance that more A4 paper was bought than A3? All reporting was disaggregated by agency and department.

The United Nations does not generate its own income from

the sale of its services or products. It is a massive "non-profit". Income is derived from donations, principally from governments, but also from non-governmental organisations, national fundraising committees and from individual donations. There are regular assessed payments from governments, like a membership fee to the UN. There are voluntary contributions for special operations – some earmarked for specific purposes and some unearmarked. All this needs to be recorded and coded in the system.

At the other end, there are investments. In order to ensure cash flow liquidity, there is always a surplus of money, which is placed into investment funds as well as short-term and long-term interest-bearing accounts. These amounts can be quite substantial, and the interest gained is additional income for the agencies.

As Thabisa had already alluded to in Turin, the income from donors and the investments are principally in large lump sums. To siphon off even small amounts, the system will flag an error. There are two locations in the system where small amounts appear, the exchange rate loss and gain and the payables. Here the system records cents, pennies, kopeks, jiao, piastre, paisa and even fractions of these, sometimes, but not always, rounded up and rounded down. It is these fractions and seemingly small amounts that can be targeted.

For example, a large non-governmental organisation, let's call them Build the School Fund, is constructing schools in refugee camps in Pakistan for Afghan refugees. BSF have a project agreement with UNHCR to build 80 schools. The budget includes buildings, furniture and educational supplies. This is all calculated in US dollars, but the expenditure is in rupees and paisa. Just to complicate matters the exchange rate for US$1 is 168 rupees one day and 171 rupees the next, but the UN exchange rate is established for several months at 170 rupees. Now, I won't bother you with the way that this is handled in the UNSFIS system, but it's messy. There are loose rupees and even paisas (which alone are pretty well useless and actually in the real world are no longer minted) all over the place.

If you are the accountant at BSF and you claim install-ments from UNHCR on the basis of receipts, denominated in rupees, for furniture, timber, roofing iron, nails and exercise books. When a lump sum of US$100,000 is transferred, are you going to check the precise amount? Any discrepancy is put down to exchange rates or even the odd accounting error.

Thabisa contacted Alejandra on the chat and between them they exchanged information. It was a slow process and took several weeks of collaboration. Alejandra needed to understand the system. They found a way in which Alejandra could access Thabisa's computer. She searched for vulnerabilities and ways to manipulate the system, a way in payables to set up a dummy supplier and tried to understand how the analytics and reporting module triggered alarms.

One of the biggest challenges that they faced was how to consolidate all these tiny amounts in almost 200 countries and transfer them to a central location. One thing was certain – they could not open bank accounts in all these countries, as bank charges and exchange rate losses would completely eat up any profit. Most digital wallet systems did not have sufficient global coverage for their purposes and, in any case, they charged a percentage fee, albeit only a few per cent, but most also required bank accounts. Most crypto-currencies would not deal in such small amounts. They even explored Western Union which had the largest global coverage, but they required a physical presence at their agencies for any transaction.

The only solution was within the UNSFIS system itself. They needed to go into the system and create a new bank account. There were hundreds of bank accounts in the system, all with their own unique code. Setting up bank accounts was by necessity a decentralised, delegated responsibility. It assumed that if you had access to the UNSFIS system, a local account could be opened. Of course, there was some security and a chain of approval. Alejandra and Thabisa spent much time sorting out a way to do this with the least possible risk. It was not foolproof, but they counted on the fact that their bank account would be lost amongst the hundreds of others. They were proud of themselves once they had worked it out, between Alejandra's IT skills and Thabisa's intimate knowledge of the UNSFIS functionality.

Alejandra then made an appointment to open a bank account at a private bank on the Boulevard du Théâtre in the banking district of Geneva, where "discretion was assured". What were once known as secret numbered accounts no longer existed, but Swiss banks do cherish their confidentiality. There are exceptions, and if you are a citizen of the United States, the Swiss banks are obliged to disclose income to the Internal Revenue Service in the United States, but Alejandra felt quite confident that she would not be unduly exposed. In any case, this was just a test account and the amounts of money she anticipated would be transferred to the account would be limited.

Alejandra was well dressed at any time, but she made an extra effort. Not only should her clothes be expensive, she needed to look (and smell) expensive. Alejandra dressed for spring on the assumption that the banker she was about to meet was male. An Oscar de la Renta white sleeveless dress with a sunflower pattern was complemented by a light cotton, yellow, Ralph Lauren blazer, to match the sunflowers. She wore camel Christian Louboutin stilettos with the red soles, visible of course, and a leather Gucci shoulder bag in camel, to match the shoes. She tied her hair back in a low *chignon* bun and sported Versace sunglasses. The pearl earrings and necklace suggested she was older than her real years. You may ask where she got the money for such extravagant apparel. No, she did not dip into her inheritance, which she probably could have if she asked. What she possesses is the art of perfecting her direct-to-consumer skills and locating last year's fashions on the web, applying her impeccable taste and, hopefully here, not making a sexist comment, she wears it all extremely well.

The bank manager she met, in a very old-worldly furnished office, was a gentleman called Aristide Genolier (on his business card it indicated by the "III", clearly proud to have the same name as his father and grandfather). There were few questions and he seemed to be happy with a post office box as an address. She could not avoid using her real name but went out of her way to suggest she was in Geneva on business and normally resided in Mexico. Monsieur Genolier did not at any time in the exchange raise an eyebrow. He, no doubt like his father and grandfather, was the essence of discretion.

Alejandra went back to her apartment, changed into her work clothes and sent a quick message to Thabisa that the account had been opened at the distinguished Banque Genolier. She carefully put her fancy clothes away so as to avoid the possibility that Gabriel may ask awkward questions. She had not shared her little extra-curricular project with him and had no intention of doing so. She arrived at the office somewhat late, mentioning that she had had a dental appointment. In any case, the UNICC worked on flexi-hours, so as long as she made up the time and was in the office for the core hours, she really did not need to make excuses.

The next day Alejandra and Thabisa made a few trial transfers. An amount of 45 piaster was an exchange rate gain from a payment made by UNFPA in South Sudanese pounds for a reproductive health clinic in Juba; 80 seniti were siphoned off a Tongan pa'anga payment to UNDP Nuku'alofa for cyclone relief materials; and 52 dinam were deducted from an instalment of 566,620.52 somoni that the ILO transferred to the Tajikistan Ministry of Labour, which was implementing a multi-year "decent work" project. There were 20 transactions in all in the total amount, once converted, of less than 50 Swiss Francs which was transferred to the Bank Genolier. Now, in a normal bank, a small amount such as this may have rung some alarm bells, but at Banque Genolier stranger things had happened frequently. They just hoped that the amounts would increase somewhat higher over time. This amount, even with the current negative interest rates would not serve the bank well.

From Alejandra's and Thabisa's perspective the trial was a success. The consolidation of small amounts and the transfer worked seamlessly, but would anybody notice and would the system flag the discrepancies? For that they needed to wait to the end of the month after the closure of the monthly accounts and after the UNSFIS reconciliation programme kicked in.

They waited. By the 10th of the next month, when the accounts reconciliation would have been completed, they checked the system and nothing seemed to be amiss. It was time to pass on the promising news to Hamiz and Kyros.

Co-option

Hamiz and Kyros were thrilled to get the message. There was much to report, so rather than chat, they had arranged a conference call. For Kyros (divorced), Hamiz (family in Pakistan), and Thabisa (unmarried), voice calls were not a problem, but Alejandra needed to take care that Gabriel was not given cause to suspect. Indeed, during the conversation, Gabriel looked in on her and may have detected a guilty look. They both worked on their home laptops after hours, Alejandra working on coding and Gabriel putting an article to bed, in order to catch the afternoon deadlines in Peru, Chile and Ecuador. Alejandra worked at a desk in the bedroom while Gabriel had commandeered the dining room table.

So, when Gabriel looked in on Alejandra and she flushed, Alejandra came up with a vague excuse about working on an interagency project. She need not have been so defensive, as for both of them working from home was the norm and generally they did not concern themselves with each other's work. She wondered whether he detected her sense of guilt. For the first time in their relationship she was not being totally honest with Gabriel. Although probably unnecessary, she resolved to tell him about an important project on which she was working and might occupy her time, requiring a degree of confidentiality, which would need to be shielded from the inquiring eyes of a journalist.

Well, back to the conversation. Hamiz and Kyros were impressed, and both exhibited an impish smile when Thabisa reported that they had already made, a so far unnoticed, profit of 50 Swiss Francs.

"Maybe we should all go out to McDonald's (virtually of course) for a Big Mac and small fries each," Hamiz suggested. "Our earnings could probably stretch that far."

"Easy for you guys, we don't have a McDonald's in Addis, which is probably for the better."

After Alejandra related her experience at Banque Genolier, Hamiz with his anti-corruption experience, expressed some concern. "I know that you had no option but to give your correct name and ID, and it was a good move to deflect on your true residence, and your disguise, which I would have liked to see, sounds impressive, but we need to find ways to ensure nothing can leave a trace back to any of us. We know that these banks are discreet, nevertheless they are often under pressure to disclose information, particularly where money laundering is suspected. Alejandra, I propose that you 'lose' your passport (he emphasised the word 'lose' so that there was no ambiguity in what was implied), and then you should apply for a new passport at the nearest Mexican Consulate. That way you can say that it was stolen, should the need arise."

"I will do that immediately. Sound advice."

Hamiz continued. "I am afraid there is an expertise gap in our plan. I know a little about offshore banking and banking secrecy, but not sufficient if we are to succeed. We need to find someone who can help us. If we earn more than 50 Swiss Francs, we cannot have it sitting in one bank. We need to move the money so it can't be traced. The money needs to disappear. We need the banking equivalent of Kyros's multi-VPN communications system. We need to make it impossible to, as they say, 'follow the money'."

"Can we trust someone else?" Thabisa said.

"Well, we did not know each other at all until Turin, yet we are putting a lot of trust in each other," Kyros responded. "I think I may have a possibility to find someone who fits the bill. If you like I can sound him out. No guarantees and I shall be very discreet. May I proceed?"

They agreed that Kyros could follow-up on his lead and report back. They had gone too far now to let the whole fishing expedition metaphorically, and using a very weak double pun, flounder on the banks.

Kyros had a neighbour in Versonnex. They both lived in the same subdivision in what the French call *jumelles,* or twin semi-detached townhouses. These are very common in dormitory France and Switzerland. They were essentially cookie cutter in design: had low maintenance small gardens or lawns front, back and one side; two floors and an attic; kitchen, dining room and salon on the ground floor with French windows to the rear garden; two or three bedrooms on the first floor with bathrooms; and an attic destined for a TV room, study or children's playroom. Kyros's neighbour lived in the *jumelle* which backed onto his property, that is to say, they shared a back fence in which there was a small metal gate. They talked regularly over the fence and frequently crossed into each other's back garden in the evening or the weekend and drank a beer or glass of wine together.

They had become good friends and enjoyed each other's company as they both lived alone. Kyros's neighbour was a widower. His wife had passed away from cancer shortly after his retirement from the United Nations Office of Geneva (UNOG) where he was the Treasurer. While notionally attached to the Department of Finance, it was a quasi-independent position reporting directly to the Deputy Director General of UNOG, who was responsible for administration and management. He invested UN agency funds, sat on the board of the UN Pension Fund, and held an advisory position with the Internal Auditors. It was a most respectable and, may I say, prestigious position.

He had been retired for six years and was looking forward to travelling with his wife, when she fell ill. He nursed her through chemo- and radiotherapy, knowing full well that there was little prospect of recovery. It was not surprising that he was somewhat bitter at this turn of events. He contemplated returning to his native Vienna, where he had worked in the National Bank of Austria, but that was so long ago that he had few friends there. Most of his acquaintances lived in the Geneva area. "Acquaintances". Yes, that's what they were. He had few real friends. There were the neighbours, fellow dog walkers, former colleagues – but these relationships never managed to transition into something deeper. They remained somewhat superficial.

His main companion now was a German Shepherd called Egon, after his favourite Austrian artist Egon Schiele. You may rightly inquire, why not Gustav (Klimt) or Oskar (Kokoschka), both of whom, he equally admired, but when he saw the dog for the first time, for some reason, he looked more like an Egon than a Gustav or Oskar. Happily, Egon was much loved and went on long walks with his master twice a day. Egon was in doggy paradise. Surrounding Versonnex there was no shortage of farmland, dissected by paved farm roads, trafficless, except for the occasional tractor or farm machinery, and extensive forests, traversed by a meandering stream. At certain times of the year the fields glowed pure yellow from rapeseed flowers and sunflowers. The walk kept Kyros's neighbour fit and Egon happy, but it was a lonely life.

The neighbour did not at all miss the work, but there was a vacuum. The morning croissant from the *boulangerie* across the road, with a strong espresso; skimming the *Tribune de Genève;* his daily walks; grocery shopping and cooking meals, a task which he enjoyed, although eating alone and not sharing the fruits of his culinary labour, gave only modest joy. Each day he looked at his emails. When he was Treasurer, he would get 70 a day on average, but these days, excluding the spam, he got fewer than 10 – and amongst them were an increasing number of obituaries of former colleagues, sent by the Department of Human Resources to all retirees. The video conversations with his children were no longer daily, as they were busy, but he saw them and his grandchildren on the weekends, which provided for a highlight after the weekday regimen.

He had expressed his lack of purpose from time to time to Kyros. He was not one to complain and made sure he did not taint his neighbour's welcome visits by that constant contagious negativity, which had a tendency to scare people away.

Egon and he were out walking in the fields late one afternoon. It was 6.30pm at the end of April. A beautiful evening on the cusp of spring and summer and still two hours of sunlight. He loved this time of year, as with each passing day the daylight hours grew longer by a minute or two, which does not sound much, but it was enough to raise his spirits. The maize was maturing, the rape flowers and sunflowers beginning to bloom. He was surprised to see Kyros out for a walk. This was a first. He wondered why, but cast that thought aside, happy in the prospect of having some non-canine company.

"Now this is a surprise, Kyros. Will you join me in our walk?"

Kyros bent down to say hello to Egon, with a friendly scratch on his neck. "Yes, that would be most pleasant. As you have realised, I rarely take a walk around here in the evening, but the fields look so welcoming. This time of year, in this area, is quite amazing. A good way to unwind from work."

"Are you busy at work?"

"Not exceptionally, but a colleague from another UN agency told me about a private project on which she is working and I can't get it out of my mind."

"Do you care to tell me about it?"

"I'm not sure it is such a good idea. She is a very good friend and what she is intending to do, while most lucrative, is certainly illegal."

"Intriguing. You can't avoid telling me now, having mystified me with that cryptic teaser."

"I think I went too far," Kyros said. "I now feel very stupid and rather rude. Please accept my apologies."

"Don't be silly, Kyros. Why don't you get it off your chest? I promise full discretion. I enjoy a good conundrum. I assure you Egon only speaks German so will not understand."

"Well, okay, but this must remain between us. My friend, who works for the UN, but not in Geneva, has come up with this harebrained scheme to siphon off money from UN agencies participating in the UNSFIS integrated finance system. It started out as a theoretical challenge in her spare time, but she tested it and it worked. Granted she only embezzled – that word sounds so degrading but I guess we need to call a spade a spade – the equivalent of 50 Swiss Francs, but that was a month ago and the loss was not picked up by the system. The scheme works on the basis that if you take a few cents or cent equivalents, never more than a dollar equivalent, from payments and exchange rate adjustments, because there are thousands of transactions, the potential income would be in the hundreds of thousands."

"*Mein Gott*, that is some system. I am not sure whether I am shocked or impressed. Probably a measure of both if I were to be honest. She must be quite a genius to come up with a way to beat the system. I am sure there are several levels of security as well as accounts reconciliation."

"Indeed, she is quite brilliant. There is just one problem. If all that money is accumulated in one bank, not only might it raise alarms about illegality and money laundering, but it can easily be traced. For the scheme to work, the money needs to seamlessly disappear."

"You have placed me in a very compromising position. Strictly speaking I should report your friend, that is if you tell me who she is, which I assume you won't. On the other hand, you have presented me with a challenge, which due to both my ego and the void of any tangible excitement in my life at the moment, I might be tempted to solve. It goes without saying, of course, that I would not do this for monetary reward" (although that temptation had also crossed his mind).

Kyros decided to remain silent. He just allowed the matter to mature, to gestate. They walked on in silence for a while. Kyros wondered why he did not take evening walks more often. This was actually rather pleasant. Egon was, no doubt, thinking about a bowl of water and maybe a meaty bone to chew. Egon's master was chewing on a thornier problem. They had made a circuit of maybe two kilometres and they were approaching their housing sub-division. Kyros was now eager to bring the conversation to a conclusion, or at least a little more advanced. That was not to be.

"Kyros, thank you for your company. I enjoyed the walk."

Was that really a reference to the physical exercise or a subtle nod to the conversation?

"It was most enjoyable for me," Kyros said. "I would like to do it again soon."

"And that we shall. I shall be visiting my son on Saturday morning for brunch, but why don't we meet in the afternoon and we can take a walk in the forest? Walking along the stream is very soothing, I find."

"That suits me well. Have a very good evening." They shook hands and Egon received a pat.

Kyros was neither unhappy with the outcome of his chat nor was he happy. His neighbour's teutonic stoicism was somewhat unnerving, but there was nothing more to be done. The seed was sown and whether a sunflower or thistle would bloom must remain to be seen another day.

Kyros sent the following message to the others: *I met my contact and explained the issue. Of course, 'I was asking for a friend' so to speak. I got a sense that he might take the bait, but it's hard to tell. We are meeting again on Saturday, and I will have some feedback for you then.*

Accountability

The UN, quite rightly, has a preoccupation with account-ability, oversight of its programmes, and ensuring a high level of integrity amongst its staff. I should not suggest that there is an overwhelming need for such bodies, although there have been instances where controls were lax and there were events that brought shame on the United Nations. There was the time after the earthquake in Haiti when peacekeepers introduced cholera to the local population. This was not intentional of course, but it took a while to admit responsibility. It was sexual abuse scandals that were the impetus for the introduction of codes of conduct throughout the system in the '90s. In one country in Africa, which I choose not to name, resettlement places were sold to refugees, profiting a local staff member. These were serious breaches of acceptable behaviour in an organisation which was expected to "do no harm". Incidents such as these are not restricted to the United Nations Agencies and were not absent from the performance of some government and non-governmental agencies working in the humanitarian and development field. And, hey, the private sector cannot remain blameless from such transgress-ions.

But, while serious in themselves and not to be excused, in the big scheme of things these incidents were not significant, and eventually were forgotten – except by the victims and perpetrators – and the balance sheet is still very much positive, in favour of the good and the honourable.

Anyway, in the '90s and at the beginning of this decade, words like accountability, ethics, zero tolerance, integrity and transparency became a frequent part of the vocabulary. Oversight bodies, Ombudspersons, ethics officers, inspector general's offices all blossomed in the UN Secretariat in New York and in the numerous UN agencies. Sometimes it was difficult to delineate responsibilities. Were they advisors, counsellors, investigators, inspectors, auditors or something else altogether? Were they representing the interests of the organisation, staff members, donors, or the beneficiaries of the agencies' good works? It would be sorted out in time – in retreats, strategic planning sessions, with the help of consultants, at interagency fora – and clarity, streamlining, restructuring, mergers, and new bodies would result, but, for the time being at least, one could be satisfied that all bases were covered.

It is now time to meet Gemma Soriano, one of these guardians of UN accountability.

Angelo Soriano was no angel, but he did work hard. Angelo drove a rented jeepney. His route started at Ayala Malls in Marikina Heights, not far from where he lived, to Pasig, some 10 kilometres south, all part of Metro Manila. He rose at five in the morning, washed the jeepney which was parked in his driveway behind a wrought iron gate, and started his route at six. Even in the '80s, the traffic was horrendous in Manila and the 10 kilometres could take one hour, and more when there were floods. He grabbed a snack from a street vendor for lunch, *kwek kwek* quail's eggs in batter or *isaw* grilled pig intestines or barbequed dried squid or other snacks on skewers, which were all easy to eat as he drove. A towel across his knees acted as a tablecloth and was useful to catch the grease and wipe away the perspiration on hot Manila days. He would not drink a lot, as toilet breaks were only possible at the beginning and end of the route, but when he did, Coca Cola was his choice. With luck the jeepney would fill to its 16-seater capacity, and he would have a sufficient turnover of passengers on the route to consider it a good day. He dreaded traffic jams, as these cut into his profits. The fares were regulated and the income only enough to earn a meagre living for him, his wife and twin girls.

Angelo cared for his jeepney like it was his third child. You could not say the same about the way he treated his wife. After a long day driving, Angelo would arrive home sometimes as late 10 or 11 at night if it was a slow day. It was left to his wife to look after the girls and he expected dinner to be waiting for him on the table. They owned the house, well almost, as the bank loan was nearly paid off. However, there were still economic challenges. This took its toll on Angelo. He was stressed and probably had feelings of guilt that he could not provide sufficiently for his family, but there was no excuse to take it out on, Maria, his wife.

Angelo was a large man, some would say obese, due to sitting all day without exercise and consuming a far from healthy diet. He was aggressive towards Maria and would beat her frequently. The twins would cower in their room and listen to music tapes on their Walkman with earphones, to block out the noise. Their mother, when asked, told them not to worry. "Dad was just stressed". There was no recourse to outside help and Angelo essentially had societal immunity. No accountability.

This was not the kind of life Maria wanted for her children, but there seemed to be no escape. Notwithstanding their home life, the twins, Gemma and Sofia, were bright – both intelligent and cheerful. They attended the Concepcion Integrated School from elementary to secondary levels. The CIS, situated in the suburb Concepcion Uno, was not too far from their house in the suburb of Concepcion Dos of Marikina. They lived in Lavender Street, in an area which strived to suggest joy, and not without irony, the neighbouring streets had names such as Rainbow, Velvet, Gold, Jasmine and Champagne.

The Sorianos lived in a modest single story cement house with a corrugated iron roof. There were just two bedrooms, the lounge-dining room, kitchen and one shared bathroom.

The property, however, had a patch of lawn out front and ample space to securely park the jeepney. Concepcion Dos was slowly becoming more gentrified, with the small modest bungalows being replaced by more modern two storey houses of fancy stonework and ostentatious balconies.

When the twins were sixteen years old, Angelo came home and proceeded to beat his wife because he was not satisfied with the meal she had prepared for him. In the course of the confrontation, Maria pushed her husband and, in spite of his bulk, he was caught off-guard and fell backwards, hitting his head on the wooden arm of the settee. Indeed, it is quite possible that his weight contributed to the impact. Gemma and Sofia, hearing the crash, rushed out of their bedroom to see their father on his back on the floor, with blood flowing freely from his head. Angelo did not move. Neither did the three women. They just stood in stunned silence and looked at each other without any hint of emotion. When Gemma and Sofia did move, it was not to check the state of their father, but to comfort their mother.

They eventually called an ambulance, and the medics were obliged to call the police. The three women stated that he tripped and fell and while the police might have suspected otherwise – this was not their first rodeo – they filed a report of misadventure.

Maria had lost a breadwinner, Gemma and Sofia a father, but any tears shed for his very few positive traits were short-lived and peace descended on number 30 Lavender Street. Maria found a waitressing job at the local Shakey's Pizza Parlour at the Marikina Heights Mall, and her teenage children were old enough to look after themselves. They excelled at school.

Sofia studied architecture and Gemma became a lawyer. It is certain that Gemma chose to become a lawyer having recognised the curse of domestic violence. She joined a neighbourhood law office in Quezon City, in which half of their cases were pro bono and half of those related to domestic violence. Both Sofia and Gemma married on the same day, at a joint wedding ceremony, at the age of 23 years. Soon after, Maria sold the Lavender Street house, at a handsome profit, to a developer and moved into a small apartment nearby. Life was looking good for Maria, Gemma, and Sofia.

Gemma was happy at the neighbourhood law office and after 10 years she was gaining quite a reputation as an activist raising awareness about domestic violence and had also become involved in domestic labour issues. She investigated the conduct of the many agencies in the Philippines which arranged for the recruitment of Filipinas as domestic workers, sent to places like Hong Kong, Dubai and London. In many cases, this was a modern form of slave labour, under a façade of legitimacy. She wrote articles, spoke at conferences and lobbied the Ministry of Labour to concern themselves with the miserable treatment of the three million Filipina domestic workers abroad. She knew it was an uphill battle, as both the families and the government valued the foreign exchange income that resulted from this human export.

To Gemma's surprise and delight she was asked, in 2011, to join the Philippine Government's delegation to the International Labour Organisation drafting conference on the Convention on Domestic Labour in Geneva. She spent three months in Geneva in drafting committees and attending plenary discussions. Yes, she was frustrated with the frequent compromises over important principles. The employer delegates were always at loggerheads with the labour union delegates, their speeches couched in platitudes and window dressing. The governments' role was often one of mediation and compromise. Progress was slow but satisfying. She felt she was at the cutting edge of a convention that would protect and safeguard the rights of so many vulnerable, mainly female, domestic workers.

Gemma was happy in Geneva and felt that the United

Nations was at the heart of global policy making. The Domestic Labour Convention did not feature prominently, if at all, in the news, but it was good news for millions of domestic workers and had a direct impact on the conditions of women. She was not so naïve to think that it would have an immediate impact on the way many employers treated their domestic helpers, but it was a first and necessary step towards that goal. What's more, it had ripples that spread way beyond Quezon City.

Even before she left Geneva, Gemma started to apply for legal positions within the UN. She did not really care where, although her preference was Geneva or New York, where she felt her input would be global and not just local. After one year, many applications, and a few virtual interviews, she hit the jackpot and was offered a job in the UN Office of Internal Oversight Services (OIOS) in New York. It was not specifically in her applied field, but it was a legal post and a new challenge was welcome.

Gemma had no trouble convincing, Mario, her husband, that the move would be a good idea. He was slowly climbing up the corporate ladder at Metrobank and Trust, but it was a large bank, and the climb could be long. He might get a job in an international bank in New York, possibly even at the Metrobank branch in Midtown Manhattan. In any case he was supportive of this opportunity which was presented to Gemma and had no second thoughts at all.

Gemma and Mario arrived in New York on a cold and miserable day at the end of November. They stayed in an equally miserable furnished apartment two blocks from the UN Headquarters. The furnishings were old and mismatched – the sort of furniture that others discard on the street and, if you are quick enough, you can grab. Yet it was very expensive, albeit within the 30-day accommodation allowance provided to new arrivals. It still hurt to fork out that much, so the hunt was on for an apartment.

There were online message boards, but would you believe that at the UN there was still a message board where employees posted cards with cars for sale and apartments to rent. That's where they found a reasonable apartment on Roosevelt Island in the East River. The cable car (New Yorkers called it a tramway) left for the island just a few blocks north of the UN building.

There are three main divisions within the OIOS: Internal Audit; Inspection and Evaluation; and Investigations. Gemma was assigned to the second and depending on the OIOS programme of work in any one year, she would inspect and evaluate the efficiency and effectiveness of agencies and programmes. She had evaluated the work of the Multidimensional Integrated Stabilisation Mission in the Central African Republic, the operations of the Office for Outer Space Affairs and progress towards the implementation of the Sustainable Development Goals with special reference to gender issues. The last one was right up her alley, but, for the first two, there was a steep learning curve. At the moment she was working on the inspection and evaluation of inter-agency joint initiatives, and this included UNSFIS.

Bank-ability

After his croissant and espresso, Kyros spent Saturday morning doing his laundry and mowing his small lawn.

His neighbour drove to Versoix, just outside Geneva, to visit his son, daughter-in-law and his grandchildren. This made him happy. Yet, he had to admit he was troubled. What would he say to Kyros in the afternoon? He could not erase the conversation from his mind, and he could not work out why. The last time he felt this way was when he fell in love. The sentiment was different, but the preoccupation, the mind games, the internal dialogue was all comparable – the temptation, the anticipation, the challenge, the excitement. He was unlikely to fall in love again in the same way as he once did, so maybe this was the challenge that was needed to bring a spark back into his life.

"Dad, Dad, you seem to be somewhere else. Is there anything troubling you? You seem preoccupied today."

"Oh, sorry I did not realise. Does it show? My mind was elsewhere. Nothing is wrong with me. It's just my neigh-bour. He has a problem," he deflected.

He drove home at noon, and at three he and Egon crossed his back garden, through the gate, and knocked on Kyros's back door, still unsure what he would say to him.

"Good afternoon. How was your morning?"

"Excellent, thank you. It's always a treat to see my children and grandchildren."

"You are indeed blessed. Shall we go? I see Egon is pulling at the leash with anticipation."

It was not far to the edge of the forest and there was a tranquil path adjacent to the stream. They took the path on the French side. In places where the stream narrowed, if one was fit enough and sufficiently adventurous, one could jump the stream and touch down in Switzerland. Egon ran ahead, rummaged and sniffed contentedly, while the two gentlemen proceeded at a leisurely pace. It was a fine afternoon, the path undulating, yet the conversation was somewhat awkward. They started with small talk: work, family, French politics, Swiss politics, world politics, the economy, the weather – each conscious that they were avoiding the elephant in the room, or should we say, in the forest. It was Kyros who needed to break the stalemate.

"Well, what did you think about my friend's dilemma?"

"I must admit, you presented me with a quandary. It's an interesting challenge, yet highly questionable in its legality. That being said, it's a subject with which I was fully engaged when I worked in the Bank of Austria. That was some time ago and although there was little need to follow the matter of offshore banking and banking secrecy in my investment role in the UN – we did everything there 'by the book' – I have continued to follow the financial and banking press quite diligently. If I may so myself, I am very much up to date on these matters."

Kyros was encouraged by the last comment. His neighbour's arrogance might just tip the balance to a positive outcome. Kyros added fuel to the flame. "I am most impressed. I am sure you are an expert in these matters, and can no doubt come up with a viable option, if not a number of options.

"You flatter me."

There was silence for a while. They walked on, each deep in their own thoughts, or attempting to speculate on each other's thoughts.

Egon sniffed, ran on and occasionally turned to confirm his master was following. For Egon, life's dilemmas were, in the scheme of things, rather small. Where to sniff, where to pee, when to hide (he liked to hear the whistle of his master), when to lead and when to follow. His challenges were manageable and his satisfaction immense. He knew the forest well, but he never tired of it.

Suddenly. "Okay, here's the deal. I'll work on your friend's problem. I will come up with a solution. There are three conditions. First, I demand full transparency. I want to know the details of the scheme and who is involved, that is, apart from you." Kyros did not need to turn – he felt the smirk. "Second, I want complete anonymity. I shall henceforth be referred to, when talking to other parties, not by name, but by a pseudonym. 'The Treasurer' would be suitable, I think. Third, you, Kyros, will be the sole channel of communication with me. Is that acceptable?"

"More than acceptable and perfectly understandable. I believe we can trust each other."

"Not too fast, Kyros. I am not yet ready to place all my trust in you, your co-conspirators, whoever they may be, nor in this venture just yet, but I hope that trust will grow once you prove yourselves. Oh, how silly of me. There is of course a fourth condition. I assume you expected this one? I am not sure yet, how many are in the 'gang', but I expect an equal share of the earnings. I do not want to get involved in the day-to-day operations. I leave that to you. You can consider my share as a retainer. I will give you banking advice initially and on an ongoing basis as required and as requested."

"An equal share is a bit steep, for an advisory role, is it not?"

"In these ventures one is recompensed according to risk and not participation. I believe, from what I have learned so far, that the risks are equivalent for all participants. This is not a matter for negotiation. Agreed?"

"Agreed." Kyros hoped that the other three would also agree. But he figured that they needed the Treasurer, they needed his good will, and the recompense would easily stretch five ways.

"Perfect. Let me invite you for tea or coffee at my place. I picked up some excellent lemon tarts at the Cartier Patisserie in Versoix this morning, which as you probably know are the best in the region. You can give me details of your team and, also, of the planning so far. I will then need just two days to come up with a viable proposal."

"Sounds good on both counts."

So, the Treasurer, Kyros, and a now somewhat exhausted Egon, walked home. Egon drank water, the big people ate tarts. Kyros told the Treasurer all he could.

The Treasurer remarked, "This is an ingenious scheme. It reflects the ideal United Nations team: multi-national, multi-gender, a good spread of skills, an excellent work ethic, clear goals and outcomes, and a high level of innovation and creativity. A textbook team, except for the integrity bit, of course. Give me two days and I shall give you a written strategy, which you will of course safeguard well and destroy once you have the system set up."

Kyros, smiled, "Sounds like a plan. We appreciate your help."

Once Kyros was back in his house, he sent a secure message to his three colleagues and reported on his discuss-ions with the Treasurer. As he predicted, they did not object to the conditions.

Two days later, as promised, the Treasurer handed Kyros a three-page document over the garden fence. Kyros retired to his patio and read the document.

I offer this advice based on my best possible under-standing of your problem. There is no certainty that it will be foolproof, and you must accept a certain degree of risk.

To the extent possible my advice comprises banking procedures which are not illegal per se, even though the source of funds is illegal and there is a clear case for considering this venture as money laundering, which is illegal.

The regulations for offshore banking and secret accounts have been strengthened in recent years. The days of easily hidden money and tax avoidance are over, but it does not mean it is not possible.

Regarding the offshore banking, there are a number of favoured offshore banking locations. What you are looking for is a combination of confidentiality, low bank charges, a low tax regime and political stability. These tax havens change over time. Last year's favourite may fall out of favour this year, particularly as more and more countries are being obliged or are willing to sign up to the Common Reporting Standards. The most secretive are probably the Maldives, Angola and Algeria, but for various reasons they are not at all popular. There is a level of instability and unpredictability and I would avoid them. Surprisingly some rich, developed countries have favourable tax regimes, for example the United States (as long as you are not a US citizen), but I would recommend the small states such as Bahamas, Cayman Islands, Panama, the Channel Islands, Seychelles and the British Virgin Islands.

You will need to set up a shell corporation so that there is a "firewall" between you as individuals and the money. This is not too complex, and I can do this for you in an effective manner.

Banking secrecy no longer really exists, if it ever did. The Swiss banks were known for their "numbered accounts", but that was often a façade as the banks did have the names and details of their clients. What they were proud of was their discretion and non-disclosure behaviour. That has been eroded in recent years. Swiss banks remain discreet but have, like most banking institutions worldwide, instituted anti-money laundering procedures and introduced "origin of funds" declarations. This may not apply to such small amounts as is expected in your scheme, but if they notice an accumulation of small amounts, it might sound alarm bells.

In that case the accumulation of substantial balances in Swiss banks may be inadvisable. I recommend using the Swiss Bank as a conduit and you should make arrangements for regular transfers to various offshore banking institutions or crypto-currencies.

As regards to your already established arrangement with the Banque Genolier, I recommend that you obscure the link between Alejandra and the bank. I understand this has been done by Alejandra "losing" her passport and applying for another. However, she will still be traceable through the Mexican passport office if the Banque Genolier so chooses, or, in the worst case, are forced by an investigative authority, to trace the owner of the account. That being said, I have made some inquiries about Banque Genolier and I am advised that they have a reputation of discretion to the extreme. So apart from a passport change, I would not worry too much about taking further precautions, except to avoid face to face contact with the bank staff and only use the bank's secure online client service feature.

This is what I propose. The small amounts are transferred into a fake holding account which you create in UNSFIS and then transferred in amounts of under 10,000 Swiss Francs to the Genolier account in Geneva. By keeping the amounts under 10,000 you will not be required to submit an origin of funds declaration. These funds will remain there for a short time. I explain later what to do with these funds. However, you should open an investment account in Banque Genolier for at least 200,000 Swiss Francs. Leave it to the bank to advise on the investment portfolio. The objective here is not to make money, but to allow Banque Genolier to accrue some brokerage fees. Indeed, if you put the funds simply in a savings account at the bank, you will lose money, as the Swiss banks apply negative interest on top of their bank fees. They will not look kindly if you use the account simply as a transit account and even an account balance of 200,000

Swiss Francs is small change for most Swiss private banks. Banque Genolier pride themselves on being a bank for high worth clients with substantial assets. You should also increase the investment portfolio with them by a substantial amount each year. A happy bank does not ask too many questions.

You should transfer the initial 200,000 Swiss Francs from a legitimate personal bank account and from a verifiable source. You will need to complete an origin of funds form (simply stating the funds result from the sale of a house, savings or wage earnings might be enough. It is unlikely they will ask for evidence, and try to avoid that so as to minimise the paper trail.) Then, when feasible, replenish your own account with funds from "the project". An origin of funds declaration should not be required if you transfer the money in small portions over time, so it will look like earnings or investment income of a high worth client.

You should transfer all your income, via Banque Genolier, to say two offshore banks and a selected crypto-currency account. Regarding crypto-currency, there are many options. I recommend Monero, which is reputed to have the highest level of anonymity and is not yet over-priced (and therefore not subject to steep value declines as others might). There remains, however, an inherent risk in putting all your eggs in one basket, particularly crypto-currencies.

As I understand it, you will accrue enough ongoing income that you will not need to bother to increase your holdings through investments in stocks and shares or investment portfolios. Doing so introduces a whole additional level of effort and complexity. Simple savings accounts, and term deposits in banks should suffice, which while subject to inflation, are not vulnerable to unpredictable market forces. Why complicate your lives?

That being said, I would be happy to make my services available as an investment broker, of course at an additional fee.

This is the overall high-level proposal. The devil is in the detail and I will help you set up the various bank accounts, including a crypto-currency account, making sure that anonymity is maximised and the paper trail is minimised. This will include, but is not restricted to, establishing temporary email IDs, burner phones for password verifications and multiple VPN addresses for online banking etc.

Kyros, this document may be shared with your colleagues, but as agreed, I shall liaise only with you in order to maintain my anonymity.

Sincerely,

The Treasurer.

Effectuation

The bits were falling into place although it was not yet the point of no return for our schemers. Kyros shared the Treasurer's letter with the other three and they were pleased with the advice so far and agreed, albeit with some misgivings, that Kyros could continue to liaise with him to implement the banking aspects of the plan. They were a little wary about the fact that the Treasurer's identity was not known to them, but Kyros said that it was clearly a take it or leave it deal. And without a viable alternative, they pressed ahead.

After a few weeks Kyros reported to them that the banking arrangements were in place. There was a crypto-currency account with Monero, and two offshore accounts were opened by a shell corporation called Quatro, which would obscure the identity of the owners; one in the Bahamas and another in Jersey. The Treasurer had arranged a mechanism whereby, using the appropriate access codes, the Four could manage the accounts. Depending on their decision, he could arrange the management of the accounts in such a way that neither Kyros, Alejandra, Hamiz nor Thabisa alone could make withdrawals or changes to the account without the agreement of one or more of the others. They agreed that any two signatories would suffice. The Treasurer and one other of the four had similar autonomy.

Alejandra followed the Treasurer's instructions and trans-ferred 200,000 Swiss Francs (most of her savings) to Banque Genolier and asked them to open a relatively non-aggressive investment portfolio. She managed all this through the online system which did not give her location.

Then Alejandra and Thabisa set about constructing the siphoning system. Thabisa created a dummy bank in UNSFIS. This was not terribly difficult. Adding new items to the large number of coding identifiers was a decentralised and simple process. For example, currency codes were pre-programmed

71

using the ISO 4217 three letter code. When South Sudan became an independent state in 2011, a new code SSP (South Sudan Pound) was created. The pound, and its units the piaster, were entered against the code. New currency codes and changes to the names and composition of national currencies are amended in the UNSFIS system centrally, by the International Computing Centre in Geneva on advice from SIX Interbank Clearing AG in Zurich, which establishes codes on behalf of the International Standards Organisation. Another code list is the UN Exchange Rate. The UN cannot change the rate on a daily basis – that would create chaos – so the so-called UN operational exchange rate is established by the UN Treasury in New York when there is a substantial fluctuation against the US Dollar. The Treasury inputs the new exchange rates in New York into UNSFIS as required.

Some codes are just too numerous to be managed centrally, and bank codes are an example. Not only are they too numerous but a globalised common identifier is not available. There are IBAN numbers, BIC/SWIFT numbers, the BSB in Australia, the CLABE in Mexico, the IFSC in India and so on. So, some heads got together in the UN and created an alphanumeric bank code specifically for UNSFIS with the three-letter country code followed by a four-digit unique number. This decentralised function allows anyone, with the appropriate clearance, to add bank codes. Thabisa had this clearance in Ethiopia and for all countries in East Africa. Codes cannot be deleted. That would cause considerable problems with system history and also be too great a risk. Imagine if someone accidentally deleted the Bank of America, HSBC, or Deutsche Bank code. Well, you get the picture, I'm sure.

Thabisa created a new bank code in Kenya. It was called the Thika Commercial Bank (Code KEN0065). She certainly did not think it prudent to choose an Ethiopian Bank, since she was based there, and she wanted a country with more than a handful of banks, so that the code would not stand out. In Kenya there were almost 30 domestic banks, 15 foreign banks with branches, the Post Office Savings Bank and some other bank-like entities such as micro-finance institutions, credit unions and insurance companies. What's more, Nairobi was an important UN Headquarters with most UN Agencies having offices there, so the volume of UNSFIS transactions was huge. Ample space for the new Thika Commercial Bank to get lost.

The good thing about the UNSFIS system was that there was a central holding account, which notionally held money in transit to and from designated banks. So, by receiving and assigning funds to a bank, the money need not physically be transferred there.

This is how it worked: Alejandra, from her position at the International Computing Centre in Geneva, programmed the system to recover all exchange rate gains of units smaller than the dollar, pound, Euro, peso and so on, and instead of moving this small change to the exchange rate loss and gain central account, moved them to the holding account for the Thika Commercial Bank. She did the same with the loose change for all the installments transferred to the implementing partners of UN programmes. The non-governmental organisations and the government departments, which implemented these programmes, would not check the cents, especially since many of these installments amounted to thousands of dollars. Another lucrative source of small change was the United Nations Pension Fund. Over 90,000 former staff are in receipt of a UN pension. These are denominated in United States dollars, but are paid out monthly to retirees in all currencies. Alejandra, not without considerable effort, and a great deal of ingenuity, found a back door into the fund and deducted an amount of the equivalent of 90 cents from each monthly payment. The annual income from this alone was just short of a million dollars.

Thabisa placed a standing instruction in UNSFIS, that when the Thika Commercial Bank's assets, in the holding account, reached the equivalent of US$9,500 it would be transferred automatically to Banque Genolier.

Once this was up and running, the transfers were made sometimes every day or even twice a day. The annual income was in the region of seven million dollars. At Banque Genolier the funds were simply moved on standing instructions and in alternating sequence into Monero crypto-currency and to the two offshore banks. From time to time, Alejandra added 200,000 Swiss Francs from the scheme's income to the investment account at Banque Genolier in order to keep them happy and she also reimbursed herself for the original personal investment.

Enough already with describing this process. Suffice it to say, that the Four were content. It was a low maintenance, highly profitable arrangement. They happily got on with their regular work, which implied that Alejandra, Hamiz and Thabisa worked hard and got good annual performance appraisal reviews, and Kyros worked as little as possible, and got mediocre performance appraisals.

Weeks passed. Months passed. Two years passed. The total accumulated funds were approaching 15 million dollars. They had agreed not to pay out a "dividend" (except reimburse Alejandra for her initial personal outlay to Banque Genolier) as their salaries were quite adequate for their needs and they did not want to draw attention to a change in lifestyle or ostentatious purchases. Even the Treasurer was content to live comfortably off his UN Pension, despite the knowledge that it was 90 cents less than it should have been each month.

Alejandra had chosen not to tell her husband Gabriel about her involvement in the embezzlement scheme. She felt somewhat guilty, but she did not want to put him in a compromising position. He had left-wing leanings, well let us say, he was highly principled. In his journalistic reporting functions, he frequently covered and reported on the functions of the Office of the High Commissioner for Human Rights, and also the annual deliberations of the Commission of Human Rights, which met for six weeks every year in Geneva. Gabriel had become increasingly frustrated with the hypocrisy of some of the 53 member states of the Commission; states, which had a poor record on human rights, some of which pontificated on the abuses of other states. The worst offenders choose not to criticise others, for fear that one day the shoe may be on the other foot. This weakened the authority of the Commission. Alejandra listen-ed to Gabriel's frustrations, nodded in genuine agreement (her political and social views did coincide with his), but she recognised her own hypocrisy. She became genuinely afraid that Gabriel may find out, and she could not be sure of the consequences.

Kyros, as has been noted, plodded on. He continued to convey to others the impression that he was busy and efficient (he made a point of walking at speed through the ITU corridors as though he was always in a hurry and thus busy) but he fooled few people. Nevertheless, he attended the ITU press briefings periodically at the main UN building, the Palais des Nations, which were usually poorly attended. Telecommunications made the news from time to time, but was usually upstaged by refugee, health, trade, human rights and even labour issues. He saw a vacancy in the public information section at the Office of the High Commissioner for Refugees once, but chose not to apply because it would likely entail far too much work. That being said, Kyros was articulate and was able to manage a press conference quite adequately. Occasionally there was a sexy issue which attracted the press corps, like explaining that 5G technology does not transmit influenza viruses, that 2.9 billion people have no access to the internet and about the cybersecurity crisis.

On 9 December he was asked to represent the ITU at an event at the Palais des Nations to commemorate World Anti-Corruption Day. This was mainly an event for staff, to reiterate the need to adhere to the UN Codes of Conduct and accountability with respect to corruption and fraud. The ITU took a keen interest in this issue, not only in relation to the expected behaviour of its own staff, but in relation to the important role that the ITU partners play in both combating corruption and ensuring they eliminate their own corrupt practices. The ITU Secretary General had asked Kyros to make a statement on behalf of the ITU and Kyros, with a straight face, yet with forked tongue, explained eloquently the importance of telecommunications entities, government or private, digital or analogue, in the rich or developing world, to not only "talk the talk, but "walk the talk".

(Yuk, I hate that expression. So clichéd, but I've heard worse in UN speeches.)

Hamiz only went home to Pakistan once in the two years since the scheme was up and running. He realised that he had little desire to see his family, but every two years he was given a lump sum to pay for home leave to Lahore, so he availed himself of the offer. He spent time with his wife, and his three children, who were growing up without him. His children and his wife found his presence in the house an intrusion. It upset the routine. They had learned to live without him. Hamiz even slept in the small guest room. It is not clear if this was agreeable to his wife or whether it was his choice. (He got his sexual pleasures from a succession of short affairs in Vienna and when these were not forthcoming, he was not shy to visit the red-light district on the Gürtel near the Vienna West train station.) His family were able to live relatively comfortably with the regular remittances he sent them, which amounted to 40% of his salary, but it never occurred to him to increase this amount or to suggest to the other three in the scheme, to withdraw a dividend, so that his family could live a more comfortable existence.

After his return from his home leave, Hamiz was asked by the Deputy Director of Human Resources if he wanted to transfer to Cairo. A position had become vacant for a Programme Coordinator for Countering Corruption and Money Laundering. The irony was not lost on Hamiz. He had become rather complacent in Vienna and thought the change might suit him well. It was not a promotion in grade, but he knew he would have more autonomy and responsibility in a country office as compared with the UNODC Headquarters. He was not sure why he was approached. Was it because no one applied for the post when it was advertised? Did they want to sideline him? Were they not satisfied with his performance? Hamiz chose to think it was because he was actually a good performer, and it was a vote of confidence. After all Cairo was an important office as the UNODC Regional Office for the whole Middle East and North Africa.

He was handed the job description, asked to look through it and give it some thought. He would, he read, "provide advice to Arab States on combating corruption and financial crime". He knew something about that. He was to "work with regional stakeholders in enhancing substantive and technical knowledge in the area of countering money laundering". Maybe here he could acquire a trick or two. Cairo was a duty station with greater hardship than Vienna so he would get home leave once a year, the cost of living was lower and the allowances substantial. He did not take long to consider this a good career and personal move, so he agreed.

Thabisa was content in Addis. The development and testing phases of UNSFIS had pretty much come to an end. There were just a few minor hiccups, but that was to be expected with an integrated system of such magnitude.

Thabisa continued to go on training missions in the region –
to Mogadishu, Djibouti, Dar es Salaam, Kampala and of
course to the UN offices in Nairobi. In Nairobi, as a single
woman alone she stayed at the Village Villa in Gigiri, the
suburb which housed the vast office complex for the multitude
of UN Agencies and many foreign Embassies. It was safer than
downtown Nairobi and her garden bungalow hotel was
modest yet comfortable and just what was needed after a long
day of training staff on UNSFIS. Even though the training had
now become second nature, it was surprisingly taxing. She
was happy to be alone. If Thabisa did not eat in the Hotel
restaurant in the evening, she would walk across United
Nations Crescent to the modern Village Market shopping
mall, where there was a choice of places to eat. One day as she
walked past a row of bank ATMs her unconscious led her to
look for the ATM for the Thika Commercial Bank. It was not
there of course, and she sniggered to herself and just for the
fun of it walked up to a stranger.

"Excuse me, do you by any chance know if there is a Thika
Commercial Bank branch or ATM in the mall?"

"I am not sure," was the ever-ready-to-please reply. "I
think I saw an ATM from that bank down the other end of the
mall just beyond the Tiramisu Coffee Shop."

"Thanks so much, I will go and look for it." She didn't
bother, although it occurred to her that a tiramisu and coffee
might go down rather well before returning to the hotel for the
evening.

In Addis, Thabisa worked hard and was well liked by her
colleagues. That said, she did not mix with them a great deal
outside of work. She worked long hours and, in the evening,
liked to read light fiction. Her only physical exercise was to
join the AAHHH, the Addis Ababa Hash House Harriers.
Now, for those readers who have not lived the expat life you
may not be familiar with "The Hash". You will find it in places
such as Kuala Lumpur (where it was invented in 1938),

Chiang Mai, Mexico City, Tonga, Accra...well you get the picture. Some say that the Hash is the drinking club with a running problem, as, after a not too strenuous run, following a trail of strips of paper, runners gather in a circle to drink. The AAHHH met, every Saturday afternoon at the car park of the Hill Town Hotel, before driving in convoy to the country-side for the run.

The first time Thabisa joined she was surprised to see so many local young ladies participating. It quickly dawned on her that they were joining in the hope to catch a UN fish of the male species. Better than walking through the deserts of Sudan and Egypt before boarding an unseaworthy boat from Libya, with sights set on the shores of Europe. Over time, Thabisa realised that she, in spite of enjoying the exercise, content with the level of socialising and barely tolerating the drinking rituals, was also not averse to the possibility that this may be the avenue for changing her status from single to married.

Inspection

Remember Gemma Soriano? Maybe you thought I had forgotten about her. As chance would have it, she arrived in Addis on a Saturday. As she pulled up to the Hill Town Hotel in a taxi, she noticed a group of expats and locals gathering in the carpark. An office outing? Never mind. It had been a long flight and she was ready to relax. UN staff were not really required to travel on the weekend when going on official missions, but Gemma usually did. While she did not like to be away from her husband, Mario, for long periods, she preferred, when travelling, to arrive on a Saturday, explore the city on Sunday and start work fresh on Monday mornings. In part this choice to travel on her time, and not that of the Office for Internal Oversight, was a result of her work ethic and dedication to the job. It was a personal choice. The organisation did not reward such diligence, but this was of no importance to Gemma.

Gemma spent the afternoon by the pool, reading her briefing notes, and chose to eat supper in the hotel's Ethiopian restaurant, since, as it was her first time in Ethiopia, it seemed proper to try the local food. She was used to eating with her hands in the Philippines, depending on the food, and enjoyed the evening meal, yet not fully finding the *ingera* totally to her liking. Sunday was spent exploring the city. She bought some Ethiopian coffee beans for Mario and some silver jewellery for herself.

So, Gemma was well rested and in good spirits as she walked (she told her contact at the ECA not to send a car) the short 10 minutes down the hill to the offices of the Economic Commission for Africa. It was a lovely morning, albeit quite cool due to the altitude. Gemma passed security and was directed to the office of the Director of Administration and Management at the tower block in the UN compound where the Economic Commission was located.

The Director, Diallo Awusu, was waiting for her in his office.

"Welcome, Ms Soriano. We have been looking for-ward to your visit. May I call you Gemma?"

Gemma knew that no one looked forward to an inspection mission, even if there were no skeletons in the closet. They were just a burden on staff time and a distraction from the routine. As for the name, a staff member at her level, did not, at least at the first meeting, contradict a Director.

"Yes, by all means call me Gemma." She was almost ready to ask whether she could call the Director by his first name, but thought better of it. "Thank you, I too am looking forward to the mission." She was equally insincere.

"Come, why don't you sit on the couch," Owusu said as he came from behind his desk.

Gemma complied but thought it unusual. She hated stereotypes, but senior staff, particularly in traditionally hierarchical societies, tended to assert their authority by remaining behind the desk. She also could not but notice that the office was not fitted out with standard UN furniture. It was not unusual for staff to add their own pictures on the walls, but this was at a whole new level. There was a large wooden antique desk, with a Georgian style wing back armchair in brown leather behind, with two matching tiffany table lamps on the desk. The floor was adorned by a Persian carpet, the filing cabinets were solid wood rather than the drab standard issue grey metal, and the sofa, to which Gemma had been directed was fronted by two matching armchairs in Biedermeier style fabrics, separated by what appeared to be a Chippendale mahogany coffee table. (Oh, I forgot to mention that Gemma liked to frequent the New York antique stores, particularly the vast Manhattan Arts and Antiques Centre on 2nd Ave, just eight blocks from her office and not at all a big detour to the Roosevelt Island Tramway on her way home. So, yes, she did know her Chippendale from her Hepplewhite and her Meissen from her Hutschenreuther.)

There was nothing in the UN rules that stated that you could not furnish your own office if you so wished, but it was highly unusual and to the extent that this office was furnished, it was equally inappropriate. The UN, at least professed to scorn elitism and foster egalitarianism. Director Owusu's office was the antithesis of what one might expect. To this seasoned inspector, a few alarm bells rang somewhere in Gemma's cerebral cortex.

She sat on the sofa as invited and to her surprise, so did Diallo Owusu. Another example of irregular and inappropriate behaviour.

"Mr Owusu, let me not waste too much of your time. You must be busy and I have a rather long standard checklist that I must complete in just five days. I would like to begin immediately if I can. Maybe we can meet at the end of my mission when you can fill in any gaps and answer any outstanding questions I might have."

"That's perfectly fine. I will introduce you to the ECA Executive Secretary and her two deputies and then I will put you in the capable hands of the Chief of Human Resources and Finance. He will manage your day-to-day schedule. Maybe we can have dinner one evening and I can show you some Ethiopian hospitality. You might enjoy a traditional *azmari bet*. There are few left in Addis Ababa, but Fendika, just along the road from your hotel is very good. You can try the local fermented drink called *tej* and listen to the haunting music."

Gemma knew where to draw the line. "Thank you, Mr Owusu, that is a kind offer, but in the evenings, I like to relax in the hotel and also spend a few hours writing up my preliminary notes." Actually, an Ethiopian colleague, who worked down the hall in Legal Affairs in New York, had recommended Fendika, and Gemma was determined to go, but not with her current company. She just had to hope she did not run into him when she went.

Gemma was pleased to leave Owusu's office. Diallo Owusu introduced Gemma to the Executive Director and the two deputies, and the usual welcomes: "we are at your disposal", "I am sure all is in order", "we have told the staff to cooperate", type comments were made. Gemma was handed on to the Chief of Human Resources and Finance and they went through the programme – which staff to see, to which files she required access and which external partners to meet. She was given a private office, as requested, so that interviews would be confidential. Then she had a collective meeting with all the section chiefs and all of the human resources, finance and general admin staff. Gemma ate lunch in the cafeteria and it was only after lunch that she got down to real work.

No, I am not going to bore you with her daily schedule. I suspect that would surely encourage you to close this book and read no further, and then, alas, the end of my story would not become known to you.

Anyway, you may recall from the very beginning of my story what happened next. Gemma was at breakfast in her hotel the next morning, when Nyala Bayene, the Finance Assistant, approached her and alerted her to Nyala's suspicions about Thabisa Maseko.

Let's cut to the chase. On Wednesday afternoon Gemma was programmed to look at the implementation of UNSFIS, but she decided that it might be strategic to meet Thabisa informally beforehand. She suggested, on Tuesday morning, that they have lunch that day in the cafeteria.

Thabisa, as was mentioned earlier, was on her guard. She knew that this was a routine inspection and that there was no reason why she should be concerned. A Finance Officer in any UN agency is in a critical position, so what's to be concerned about? Of course, what Thabisa is not aware of, was the encounter between one of her assistants and Gemma after breakfast that morning.

"Thanks for meeting me over lunch," Gemma started. "It's

always good to meet informally and anyway I find that eating alone while on mission is not very pleasant."

"My pleasure. My life here consists of work and little social interactivity, except for one social event each week and the regional training missions. I certainly sympathise with you about the loneliness while on mission, having undertaken many myself in the region."

"How is the UNSFIS implementation going? I understand you are the regional focal point?"

"It was complicated at the beginning. Change always is. There was much resistance, and the system had many teething problems. But now it's all pretty much sorted and it seems to be running smoothly. I suspect that the training missions will end soon."

"You have been here five years as I understand it, Thabisa. Are you thinking of applying for positions in other duty stations? You are probably ready for a promotion to a higher grade, which seems unlikely here."

Thabisa, subconsciously, noted the shift from UNSFIS to Thabisa's personal situation. Was this small talk or Gemma's investigative persona in action? "Actually, in spite of the routine, I like it here. I am invested in seeing UNSFIS a success." Whoops, maybe a poor choice of words.

"Hmm, interesting." Gemma paused and there was a momentary silence.

Thabisa was unnerved. She changed the subject. "How do you find the hotel?"

"Fine, thanks. It's perfectly comfortable and I like the pool and gardens. It's similar to most hotels that I have stayed in on my missions. They become very impersonal. I enjoy getting out a bit to explore, particularly in new cities. In fact, I was told that one special evening activity here is to go to an *azmari bet* for the music. Do you know the Fendika?"

"Indeed yes. It's just a short distance from my apartment in Kazanchis and close to the Hill Town Hotel. I have been once or twice. Shall we go this evening? I would be pleased to accompany you there. I could meet you in the hotel lobby at eight and we can walk there. How does that suit?"

"I would like that very much. Thanks."

Gemma and Thabisa hit it off, even though Thabisa remained somewhat anxious. They talked about their respective upbringing in the Philippines and South Africa and compared married and unmarried life. They parted on good terms.

At eight that evening, as arranged, Thabisa met Gemma in the lobby and they walked the 15 minutes to the Fendika. It was already dark, but they kept to the main road, which was well lit, and busy with pedestrians and traffic.

The Fendika consisted of a few spaces with a reception area and bar and the main room where the music took place. It was decked out like a large Bedouin tent – Ethiopian handwoven cotton embroidered fabrics adorned the walls, straw was strewn on the concrete floor, the seating was intimate, close to the musicians and close to other patrons in a semi-circle around the performers. Gemma and Thabisa were directed to low leather stools at a small coffee table.

"I recommend you try the *tej* for the authentic experience." Thabisa proposed. "It's made of fermented honey and a special herb. It is an acquired taste. I will get some from the bar."

As she left the bar Thabisa spiked Gemma's drink with a small dose of poison she had purchased in the market after work. She had not been certain she would use it. It was a contingency, yet she did indeed find herself crossing that line. As she returned to Gemma, she had second thoughts and was about to tip out the bottle and get another, yet contrary to her conscience, she continued and handed the bottle with the golden liquid to Gemma. "Here you are, Gemma. You drink directly from the bottle. I hope it is to your liking."

Gemma did not like it much but drank. The Ethiopians in

the room drank *tej* or the local Hakim Stout or St George Amber Beer.

The music was indeed haunting, the screech of the *masenko*, the single string instrument played with a bow, somewhat mesmerising. The male singer, the *azmari*, was clearly chanting a poetic story to the music and periodically the audience laughed at the humour or double-entendres.

They stayed for about two hours, but not under-standing the linguistic craft of the *azmari* prevented it from being a complete experience. After two bottles of *tej*, Gemma was feeling a little dizzy. She took a taxi to the hotel and Thabisa walked the few blocks home.

Gemma had a terrible night. She must have found her face over the toilet bowl at least every hour. In the morning the hotel arranged for the house doctor to examine her and recommended at least two days in bed, drinking lots of tea. He was sure it was food poisoning and would go away with time.

Gemma's mission needed to be aborted as she had to get back to New York for an important strategic planning session and could not possibly make up the two lost days in Addis. She left on Friday not having set foot in the office after her evening with Thabisa.

On Friday morning, there was a knock on Thabisa's door. It was Nyala, one of the finance assistants.

"Good morning, Nyala. How can I help?"

"I know what you are doing. I'm not stupid. I was doing the bank reconciliation at the end of last month and I noticed an exchange rate discrepancy in the quarterly installment to the African Union Development Agency Climate Resilience Project. It was not a lot but when I looked at the instalments to IIED, ACGSD, GBV/VAW, IGAD and a few other imple-menting partners I found a similar discrepancy."

"Nyala, what's so unusual with that? There are always exchange rate gains and losses."

"Yes, I know, but the gains were not coded correctly, and I

cannot find the gains in the exchange rate loss/gain account."

"Thanks, Nyala, for sharing this with me. No need to do or say anything. I will look into it."

"No, I thought you may say that, and it confirms my suspicion. I think you are stealing from the organisation and I also think you poisoned the inspector from the OIOS."

Thabisa was taken aback, but maintained her calm composure. "What an outrageous accusation. You do realise that such a false accusation could lead to your dismissal?"

"And any hint of fraud could lead to yours," was Nyala's retort. She was feeling confident and felt she now had the upper hand.

"Hmm, it seems we have a standoff. Nyala, I like you and you have been a good staff member, but I am afraid I do take your accusation personally. I have not done anything wrong, but I could no longer work with you after such an outrageous accusation. Embezzling funds. Poisoning a colleague. Really? I am not sure anyone would believe you. What they might believe, however, is that you have been having a sexual relationship with Diallo Owusu. Now that is highly improper and contravenes the Code of Conduct, not to mention acceptable moral norms. The Director is a married man." The last bit was unnecessary, but Thabisa wanted to not only insert the knife but twist it in the wound.

Nyala flushed. She was stunned. Not just that she was exposed but also that mild and gentle Thabisa would be so blunt. Now Nyala was on the defensive and there was an awkward silence.

Thabisa filled the silence. "I will tell you what will happen. You will hand in your resignation, for family reasons. I will write you an outstanding performance appraisal and a glowing reference. You will easily get a job at another agency or elsewhere, but not here at the ECA as long as I am here. With a bit of luck, I will move on in a year or two. In the meantime, you will forget your silly accusations, because if the knowledge of your sexual liaison with Owusu becomes public, your prospects of getting another job in the UN will be pretty much zero. You may go now. You have a letter to write."

Nyala, tears clearly welling, left the office. Thabisa felt rotten. She had stooped so low. Her role in the embezzlement somehow did not keep her awake at night, but poisoning and blackmail, that was at another level altogether.

By the time Gemma's 18-hour flight via London landed in New York she was feeling perfectly fine, albeit very tired. It was late Friday evening in New York, but time for breakfast in Addis. She took a taxi to her home, woke Mario as she crawled into bed, gave him a hug and a kiss and tried to fall asleep. She did little on the weekend except go to the doctor and have a blood test. On Monday the test results showed that indeed she had had food poisoning, but the source could not be determined. Over the weekend Gemma had plenty of time to think. Was there something to Nyala's accusations? She liked Thabisa, and could not believe she was doing anything wrong, but there was still that niggling feeling.

You may recall, but I won't at all be surprised if you don't, that the OIOS in New York has three divisions: Inspection and Evaluation (that's where Gemma works); Internal Audit; and Investigations. Internal Audit was on the floor below the one where Gemma worked and before the strategic planning session began on Monday, she walked down to her audit colleague, Ekaterina Kutznetsov.

"Hi, Katya, have you got a few minutes?"

"Of course, Gemma, I always have time for you."

"I'm not sure if I am imagining things, but I had a strange experience in Addis last week. I went there on a routine inspection mission." Gemma related the events: meeting Nyala and the far-fetched possibility that she was poisoned to force her mission to be aborted. "Katya, I do not want to go so far as to request a formal audit based on my experience, but is there any way you could do a spot audit on UNSFIS?"

"Indeed, a full audit is highly unlikely now, Gemma. We have an audit of UNSFIS scheduled in our workplan in two years' time. For that we will have a team of six auditors who will do nothing else for a whole year. In my opinion UNSFIS is a monster and should never have been contemplated. The decision to create it was certainly not made by an accountant, but by a bunch of dreamers on the 16th floor or in one of those inter-agency think tanks where the best and brightest get together and develop utopian schemes that require the best and brightest to implement. There is just one flaw in that approach – it assumes that it will be implemented by the best and brightest. But that's not always the staffing reality in the field."

Gemma dearly loved Katya, except for her propensity to go off on a tangent, criticising senior decision making. She may have had a point, but UNSFIS was a reality and it was too late to turn the clock back. This was certainly beyond Katya's sphere of influence and her pontificating was wasted energy.

"Is there nothing you can do?"

"I'll tell you what. I will do some random spot checks into the accounts. I can't promise anything will turn up, but give me a week or two and I'll let you know."

"Thanks Katya, I owe you a nice dinner. Mario and I will take you and Alexi to the new Greek restaurant on the corner of 52nd and 3rd. It's supposed to be excellent."

Two weeks passed and Katya called on Gemma.

"Gemma, I did what I could squeeze into my already busy schedule. I looked to see if there were any large sum anomalies in the global reconciliation account and could find nothing. That does not mean some large lump sums were not siphoned off. To be sure I would need to audit each country's set of accounts and that is just unfeasible for me at this stage. I then looked at a random selection of UNSFIS bank accounts to check for any oddities. If there is a case of fraud or embezzlement, one place to look is the bank accounts. That's a massive task of course. Worldwide there are thousands of bank accounts, some administered by each of the UN agencies and others which receive money from the UN for their implementation activities. Many are very active and a large number dormant. I checked a selection and found nothing irregular. Of course, I cannot rule out that the governmental or non-governmental partners are not siphoning off funds after installments are transferred to them, rather than using it for the benefit of our joint projects. For that we would need to audit their books. In any case Thabisa, the Finance Officer, would need to be in league with these partners and I found no indication of that although it cannot be ruled out. I am sorry, but I found no evidence of wrong-doing."

"Well, I guess that's about as far as I can go. Thanks, Katya." Gemma was somewhat disappointed, yet to some extent relieved that there was no smoking gun. That said, it was a too big an ask of Katya. Maybe she was right, Gemma thought, in UNSMIS we had created a monster.

Disintegration

Strange things, proverbs. Do "many hands make light work" or do "too many cooks spoil the broth"? No, you can't have your cake and eat it. This saga could be called "nothing ventured, nothing gained", and that's how it began. But soon, it seemed, that "all their chickens came home to roost".

I guess the cracks started to appear in Addis when meek and mild Thabisa, nice, friendly Thabisa, slipped something into Gemma's *tej*. Yes, she felt guilt. *This was not me*, she thought. And then, what's more, she orchestrated the resignation of Nyala. Was it the desire for money? Was it the fear of getting caught? She had risen from the townships, managed against all odds to get a good education and now she had a good professional position in the United Nations. The United Nations! Her parents were proud of her. A day did not go by when, back in Giyani, Nomusa Maseko did not remind a neighbour, or Themba Maseko did not comment to a fellow worker at the open pit copper mine, where he drove a front-end loader, that their daughter worked for the United Nations. Actually, was that the reason why Thabisa acted so irrationally? Maybe she simply did not want to disappoint her parents.

Some weeks later, Nyala left the ECA, not before the obligatory farewell party, in which Thabisa, as her supervisor, gave a glowing speech. Thabisa praised her efficiency and competence and said that she was sincerely sorry to see her go. Looking directly at Diallo Owusu, Thabisa said Nyala was a good friend to all staff and that she will be sorely missed by colleagues. Nyala, feigning shyness, chose not to respond in spite of the invitation to say a few words.

Thabisa, acknowledging her own duplicity, needed to confide in someone. There was only one option. The next morning, a Saturday, Thabisa broke the cardinal rule and called Alejandra in Geneva on Skype rather than the secure chat that Kyros had set up. Was this a sign that the unity of the Four was developing some cracks? This was not the time for chat messaging. She wanted to see a friendly face and also did not want Kyros or Hamiz to be privy to their conversation.

"Hi, Alejandra. Is this a good time to talk?"

"Perfect. How lovely to see you. How are you?"

"Well, that's the reason I called. Not so good."

"What's up? Are you ill?"

"No, nothing like that. An inspector from OIOS came to Addis. It was a routine inspection mission, but I got a sense that she was suspecting something was fishy about my accounts. We went out to a bar in the evening, and I slipped poison into her drink. I was careful and she only got a bout of what she thought was food poisoning, but it had the desired effect. Her mission was aborted and she returned to New York."

"I am amazed at what you did. It's not like you, but well done. Do you think there is still a risk?"

"Possibly, as it did not end there. My finance assistant accused me of embezzlement and also poisoning the inspector. I think she was the one who reported me. I managed to neutralise that threat, as I knew she was sleeping with one of the directors. I asked her to resign, or I would expose the affair."

"Wow, Thabisa, you really are a surprise. What do you think we should do? Take our earnings and cut and run?"

"No, Alejandra, I think for now we are okay. The finance assistant may find a way to get revenge. I probably would if I were her. I do not think she has any hard evidence, or she would have given it to the inspector. Let's continue. The scheme is certainly working like clockwork and the income is still several hundred thousand a month."

"Thabisa, thanks for sharing this with me. I can imagine the last few weeks have been hell. Can I do anything?"

"No, I just wanted someone in whom I could confide. I

cannot keep it all bottled up. I know I am a changed person. It's good to have you as a friend."

"You flatter me, but thank you. Anyway, as we say in Spanish: *Agua pasada no mueve Molino;* water that has passed does not turn the mill wheel. I guess you would say, 'that's water under the bridge'. At least let's hope it is."

"Me too. Thanks for listening. I feel more at ease now."

"I am actually pleased you called. There are two things that I want to share with you. The first is, I am not sure that I can trust Kyros. So far all is going well, but a week or so ago I happened to be at the World Anti-Corruption Day event at the Palais des Nations. It was mainly a staff event, with a few representatives from the Permanent Missions to the UN and some NGO representatives. We sat through the inevitable and predictable speeches. Kyros was there and spoke on behalf of the ITU. Not bad really. Short and well delivered. I was with a friend, who happened to be from the ITU and she mentioned that he was 'dead wood' and she thinks he will be separated from service. My friend was not aware that I knew him. I am worried what he may do if he is dismissed. The way the scheme is set up, he and the Treasurer, with whom only he is in contact, could empty out the accounts. We need to keep an eye on that."

"Indeed, the whole arrangement relies on trust. I think if he is separated from service, we should all agree to take a dividend. That may pacify him. As long as we all agree to no sudden lavish spending."

"Makes sense."

"What's the second thing?"

"This one is a little more personal and maybe more problematic, but I am happy to confide in you. Gabriel accused me of having an affair. He wonders why I am having confidential conversations. I found it very hard to lie to him. He is, as you know, a journalist, and a good one. He is able to read faces well, and sometimes I think minds. He is an expert at asking questions, which at times feels like interrogation. Things got very tense and he knew I had a secret. We had vowed not to keep secrets from each other, and the guilt mounted. I caved. I told him that I had stolen some money from the UN. I did not go into detail and I certainly did not tell him that it amounted to millions of dollars. I realise in retrospect I should have admitted to an affair. I am not sure what he would have found more troubling. He certainly, I found out, drew the line at theft, especially from the UN. I tried to explain that it was just a challenge to see if it was possible. An exercise in possibility and capability. Sadly, he did not buy it. We now live apart and I suspect he will want a divorce. I am shattered, but whatever excuses I now make fall on deaf ears. Communication between us has completely collapsed."

"I am so sorry, Alejandra, really I am. Maybe we should indeed stop the scheme?"

"I am afraid it's too late. I cannot convince him to come back. Let's monitor it for a month or two more, but I think it will be time soon to pull the plug."

"Agreed. We'll talk again in one month."

"Fine. Looking forward. Bye, bye."

Now, I shouldn't give you a lesson on the activities of the UN Office on Drugs and Crime Regional Office for North Africa and the Middle East, to which Hamiz had been reassigned. But, hey, why not? At least I will report the events as I was aware of them or at least imagined them. This is, after all, a story about crime and I should at least tell both sides – the good, the bad, and the ugly. Okay, three sides.

Soon after Hamiz had arrived in Cairo as Programme Coordinator for Country Corruption and Money Laundering, he discovered that job descriptions were rather flexible. On his first day, he was welcomed and briefed by the Director of Programmes and Operations at the UNODC office in Maadi, in the southern suburbs of Cairo. The Director was most courteous.

"Hamiz, welcome to Cairo and the region. We are very pleased that you have joined our team. How have your first days been?"

"So far so good. I feel very much at home in the city. In many ways it's not unlike Lahore. I am staying in the Villa Belle Epoque, which as you know is not far from here. I think it was recommended by the office to give me a soft landing. It certainly is true to its name. Of course, I should find an apartment quickly. I have the name of the estate agent the office uses and it seems that there is plenty of choice. I shall look around the office, as I like the area and it is good to be a little removed from downtown Cairo."

"Excellent. Let me know if I can do anything, but we have a good admin team and you will be in efficient hands."

"Thank you."

"Now, if you permit me, we shall get immediately down to business. I am a little embarrassed. Between the time you were appointed and your arrival we have reviewed our projects and the office's strategic plan. A number of donors, on whom we have relied, have withdrawn funding, but others have been forthcoming. Some of our priorities have changed and we are trying to realign staff competencies. I am not sure how wedded you are to Corruption and Financial Crimes. I note it is not your precise expertise and that you have been involved in a range of areas in Vienna. Our other programmes are Crime Prevention and Criminal Justice; Prevention of Drug Use; Countering Terrorism; and Combating Organised Crime. It is the last of these for which we have a staffing gap and to which we would like you to be assigned. The crux of this programme area is dismantling human trafficking and migrant smuggling networks in North Africa, particularly

Egypt, Libya, Morocco, and Tunisia. I understand your Arabic is fluent and I am sure that you can work well with the various governments and implementing partners. As you know this is an incredibly delicate priority concern of the donors, particularly in Europe. What do you think?"

Hamiz was sufficiently astute to realise that this was a rhetorical question. The Director was simply going through the motions to sell a decision that was probably non-negotiable. It was not the time to object, and anyway it sounded quite interesting. He knew it was a priority for the UNODC, and the European donor interest, he knew, was a euphemism for "keep the migrants and refugees in Africa. We don't want them coming to Europe". They were ready to pay UNODC to support their policies of offshoring their own responsibilities as countries of asylum.

"I am happy with that programme," Hamiz replied with an adequate level of enthusiasm. I am here to serve the office in any way I can." Maybe he laid the latter on a bit thick.

"Excellent. Tomorrow, we have our regular weekly meeting with all five Programme Coordinators and the programme staff in their respective sections. You will meet the other four coordinators tomorrow. It is rare that all five are in Cairo at the same time.

If Hamiz was to be honest, UNODC ran some pretty sensible programmes. They were swimming against the tide (an unfortunate metaphor) on combating people smuggling and trafficking across the Mediterranean. And on drugs, financial crimes, organised crime, corruption and terrorism it was an equally uphill battle, but these were issues that could not be ignored, and any small breakthroughs were noble, even if it was a two-steps-forward and one-step-back, or even a one-step-forward and two-steps-back proposition.

He liked his colleagues. All seemed very professional and dedicated. After the meeting, the Director took him aside and, again apologising, said there was an important EU delegation visiting Libya and he should go there on mission immediately. He was to meet up with the other UN agencies and join the meetings with the EU delegation, a group of Ministers of Internal Affairs from Sweden, Germany, Italy and Spain. A serious delegation. The smuggling and trafficking activities out of Libya had received much criticism and something needed to be done. The EU governments, particularly Malta and Italy, were being criticised for push backs of rescue vessels operated by some NGOs, and the others criticised for their lack of burden sharing. Germany was one of the more welcoming governments, but even they were finding that their domestic constituencies were starting to react negatively to an influx of asylum seekers.

The next afternoon Hamiz was already on a plane for the short hop to Tripoli. He took a taxi to the Hotel Al-Safwa. It was not the most salubrious of hotels, just 3 stars, but it was recommended due to its proximity, just across the square, from the United Nations building in Tripoli. This was his first visit to Tripoli, so he decided to go for a walk and get his bearings while there was still some light. Hamiz walked the short distance to the harbour and turned left towards the Public Garden, which he traversed to Martyr's Square, down Independence Street, past City Hall, and back to the hotel. Not a very long walk, but welcome nevertheless. He grabbed an early dinner in the mediocre hotel restaurant and read some briefing notes before turning in. Such a typical routine. Another city. Another rather unattractive hotel. A lonely walk. A solitary meal. Another night in an unfamiliar bed.

After breakfast, Hamiz crossed the square to the UN building where he met the only UNODC staff member in Libya, a locally recruited liaison officer. Hamiz did not have a lead role in this mission, which was probably a good thing, as he was unfamiliar with all the issues in Libya. The UN delegation was headed by the UN Refugee Agency (UNHCR) and the International Organisation for Migration (IOM), whose representatives seemed to compete for primacy. The first meeting took place in the Embassy of Italy, partly because they had good conference room facilities, but primarily because Italy held the current presidency of the European Union.

There was, as Hamiz had expected, a difference of opinion between the EU government representatives and the UN. The meeting was cordial, in a rather stilted and formal way. The UN officials, stated as diplomatically as possible that they were concerned about the stance of the European governments not allowing asylum seekers, who cross the Mediterranean, landing facilities in Italy and Malta. For their part, the diplomats stated, in undiplomatic terms, that it was acceptable to assist countries of origin to hinder departures, and countries of transit to detain them. What they could agree on, was that the shelter facilities, most of them detention centres, did not comply with acceptable minimum standards.

Hamiz realised that he should intervene and knew enough to express UNODC's concern over the problem with smuggling, trafficking, exploitation, sexual abuse and rape, and the fact that many of the centres housing migrants and refugees were run by criminal groups, militias and gangs.

The afternoon was spent visiting some of these centres. The press was kept at arm's length at the request of the government ministers. These were not pretty places and photo opportunities juxtaposing well-dressed diplomats with bedraggled detainees would not have gone down particularly well.

Hamiz had a restless night. Who in their right mind could sleep after what he had witnessed that afternoon? The squalid conditions, in disused factories and run-down, unsanitary, overcrowded facilities. The smell hit him wave-like as he entered these vast people warehouses, sleeping mats side by side, barely a foot space between. There was no privacy nor protection, especially for women and children. Faces were full of fear, staring in the distance, at a future dashed and out of reach. For the first time, Hamiz, who was selfish and greedy, who treated his family as if they were a burden, an irritant, a drain on his personal income (not to mention the bulging bank account), could not jettison an inkling of guilt. He detected in himself a change, maybe not a watershed, but a change nevertheless.

What about Kyros? Was he eventually fired? The Director of External Relations and Communications at the ITU would have dearly liked to replace him. He knew he would get greater productivity out of pretty much any replacement. Indeed, he used the term "dead wood" frequently to the other Directors. He wrote mediocre performance evaluations, but they were just not bad enough for dismissal on the grounds of poor performance. When money was available for another communications officer post, at one level higher than Kyros, the Director recruited a younger person from outside the UN System. Kyros took a case to the UN Administrative Tribunal. According to the staff rules, internal staff with "adequate" performance appraisals and the requisite seniority at the current grade took precedence over external recruits. Kyros won the case and was promoted. The director was furious, but could do nothing, except make life hell for Kyros.

Kyros became very depressed. He should have resigned, but life in Geneva had become too cosy. He had a good salary and although the cost of living in Geneva was high, he lived comfortably. He could visit Greece easily and with six weeks of vacation days each year plus the statutory holidays, he had the time and savings to travel. It just seemed easier to stay than to look for another job and disturb this complacency. Of course, there was also a small matter of his share of now over 14 million dollars in unearned income, but the agreement was not to take a dividend for at least another 12 months. He thought that when the payoff did come, he could retire to a villa on Mikonos or Paros and watch the fishing boats arrive with his dinner.

The Treasurer, meanwhile, was perfectly happy. Walks with Egon, visits to the grandchildren, plenty of time to read and a few train journeys to a surfeit of superb destinations in France, Switzerland and Northern Italy. He was attracted to the wine districts of the Langhe and Burgundy, and in the winter, he cherished the peace and fresh air, snowshoeing in the Jura Mountains. Both the wine and the snowshoeing were taken in moderation, the former to ensure continuing good health, the latter due to normal age-related fitness. For him, life was rosy.

Oh. I nearly forgot. There is one thing you should know, to which Alejandra was not privy. Gabriel was more upset than she could ever have imagined. He became very troubled. It was two in the morning as he tossed in his bed and could not get back to sleep. He got up and booted up his computer. He googled: "Investigation of UN staff misconduct". First hit:

Office of Internal Oversight OIOS

https://oios.un.org.

Where evidence of misconduct is established, the Investigations Division will respond to confidential reports of waste, fraud, mismanagement, or other wrongdoing in the United Nations.

He entered. A big red box with the words REPORT WRONGDOING was not shy to jump out and below a phone number in New York with a 24-hour hotline. It was eight in the evening in New York. Why not? He called. After he put the phone down, he was overcome with guilt. But, too late, it was water under the bridge.

Investigation

At this point, Malcolm Malouf enters our story. I guess I will go back to his beginnings, as it might help you become familiar with what makes him tick.

On 11 November 1975 the Governor General of Australia did something that had never been done before. On that day he dismissed the Labor Prime Minister, Gough Whitlam and appointed the Liberal Party leader, Malcolm Fraser to the post. This event was front page news in the *Toronto Globe and Mail*, *The Hindu Times*, the *Washington Post*, *The Guardian* and practically every other major newspaper worldwide. On that Tuesday, in the birth announcements on page 22 of the *Sydney Morning Herald*, and only the *Sydney Morning Herald*, was the announcement of the birth of Malcolm Malouf.

Ten years later, Malcolm Malouf asked his father, Sameed, why he was named Malcolm.

"You were named after Malcolm Fraser, the Prime Minister of Australia. I wanted you to have a name typical of an Australian so that you would not be teased when you grew up."

When Malcolm was 20 years old, he asked his father. "Father, why did you call me Malcolm and not Gough. Aren't you a Labor Party supporter?"

"I could not pronounce the name Gough. What sort of name is that?" was the reply.

Malcolm Malouf was born in Punchbowl, a suburb in the midst of the sprawling southwest of Sydney. It, like its neighbouring suburbs, was not the most salubrious of locations, but it is not ugly nor run down either. The streets form, more or less, a grid around the relatively compact town centre, which is just a one kilometre stretch of single-storey shops, small businesses and service offices. The houses sit on quarter-acre blocks (yes, they do use hectares, but for historical reasons the quarter-acre block nomenclature is ubiquitous). There are three-bedroom bungalows of brick with grey tiled rooves or two-storey flats (known elsewhere as apartments) of brick with grey tiled roofs. If you were to eavesdrop through a house window in Punchbowl, you would have only a 30 per cent chance of understanding what is said, unless you happen to understand Arabic, Vietnamese, Italian, Greek, Bengali, Urdu and Cantonese.

Like many of the residents of Punchbowl, Sameed and his wife, Hamia, migrated to Australia from Lebanon. There were several waves of Lebanese migration and Sameed and Hamia chose to leave Lebanon in 1968, shortly after the Six-Day War and before the major influx, which followed the Lebanese civil war in 1975, the year that Malcolm was born. Suffice it to say that Malcolm grew up amongst Lebanese, spoke Arabic at home, and was as fond of hummus and falafel as he was of a Big Mac or the standard "meat and three veg".

Malcolm went to Punchbowl Boys High School, a short walk from the family home. Today it is considered an excellent school and can rightly boast the achievement of the school motto: Dream More, Learn More, Do More, Be More. But it was not always so. When Malcolm attended in the late '80s there were serious discipline problems and drugs were freely available. Malcolm did not deal, and he was not the worst abuser, but he was on the verge of a downward spiral when one of his teachers recognised a spark of potential, took Malcolm under his wing and somehow managed to gain Malcolm's confidence. His teacher redirected Malcolm's attention to study and sport. Malcolm was a good sportsman. He was tall and strong and played Australian Rules football and joined the local boxing club.

Malcolm continued "footy" and boxing at university. He was encouraged by his mentor to escape Sydney and take a course at Charles Sturt University in Bathurst, in rural New South Wales. He chose a basic humanities course but did not fully cherish academic studies. Nevertheless, Malcolm graduated with a (mediocre) Bachelor of Arts degree and decided to attend the New South Wales Police Force Academy in Goulburn, which had an association with Charles Sturt Uni.

After some years as a beat policeman and then an investigator, he was deployed with the Australian Police Force to the United Nations Interim Force in Lebanon (UNIFIL) as a truce observer. Now here is a misnomer if ever there was one. UNIFIL, which still operates today, was established in 1978 – not much "interim" about that. This deployment served Malcolm well as he could improve his Arabic and discover his roots. In 2015 he was offered a position in the UN Department of Peacekeeping Operations (DPKO) in New York, advising UN member states on rule of law issues as they relate to police matters.

It was a miserable day. Malcolm walked the two blocks from his one-bedroom apartment in Tudor City up 1st Avenue to his office on the 27th floor of One UN Plaza. The rain was fierce – horizontal rain – making a frontal assault on pedestrians on the Avenue. A little time later, he was staring out the window at the iconic United Nations Headquarters building and beyond it, to the East River. He had finished his espresso and croissant purchased, as was his habit, from the coffee cart situated on the forecourt of the UNICEF building on E 44th Street. He had scanned his emails – deleted some, replied to very few, filed others in his "to do" folder and left others to just fester in the inbox, either letting the passage of time take care of them or await a gentle follow-up asking whether "he had had a chance to look into the matter". He had scanned the *New York Times*. He had reviewed his daily agenda of meetings, of which there were only three.

He kept staring out the window because he just could not

generate the energy to write the long overdue mission report from his trip to Haiti to evaluate the since terminated United Nations Mission for Justice Support in Haiti (MINUJUSTH), which, amongst other tasks, supported Government efforts to further develop the Haitian National Police.

With a smile, he recalled the joke:

Q. "Why don't international civil servants look out the window in the morning?

A. "Because if they did, they would have nothing to do in the afternoon."

Not really fair, as most of his colleagues worked hard, and some worked very hard, but the joke always prompted a chuckle.

A knock on the door startled him somewhat. His boss invited herself in and took a seat.

"Malcolm, I have been approached by the Office of Internal Oversight across the road. They are short-staffed and are looking for an investigator for a six-month secondment. They approached us. What have you got pending?"

"Nothing much. I just need to complete the mission report from the Haiti mission. It should require just one more day to do that. After that there is just routine work."

"How would you like a change of scenery. I am not sure what they have in mind or whether travel is involved. Interested?"

"No worries. Suits me." Malcolm, like most of his compatriots, was pretty laid back about most things.

Malcolm completed his mission report as planned. He was conscious that the UN was still getting much criticism for its handling of the cholera outbreak introduced in 2010 by Nepalese peacekeepers serving the UN Stabilisation Mission in Haiti (MINUSTAH), the predecessor of MINUJUSTH. Malcolm was aware that he should sing the praises of MINUJUSTH, although its rather focused mandate and specific achievements could not erase the death from cholera of 10,000 Haitians.

The next day at 8:30am, Malcolm crossed the road to the main UN building. After passing the security gate with his UN badge, noticing that security was tighter than normal, Malcolm stopped at the lobby café for an espresso and cream cheese bagel. As his appointment was at 9:30am, he had time to watch the passing parade of UN staffers, delegates and diplomats from the country permanent missions to the UN. The lobby was more crowded than usual and he realised that it was the second day of the annual high-level session of the General Assembly. Presidents and foreign ministers joined local ambassadors for their speeches to the plenary. As he watched the delegates with their entourages and minions passing by with demonstrable importance, and at times personal security, Malcolm reflected on his presence in the centre of it all. Here was the focus of international politics and diplomacy. Well, there was not much of the latter at times. Annual recurring squabbles between Morocco and Algeria, between USA and Iran, between Israel and the Palestinians, between Myanmar and Bangladesh and so many more harsh words spoken between nations, not in jest. He often watched the television news in the evening and thought "I was there today" or "look, there's my office across the road behind that CNN, BBC or Al Jazeera talking head".

It was a far cry from Punchbowl back in Sydney. Malcolm often wondered whether the short order cook at Chubby Buns Burgers or the recently immigrated greengrocer and his wife, who between them worked 24/7, at Always Greener Fruit and Groceries on Canterbury Road, Punchbowl, really cared what went on in the General Assembly. Why should they? These were two very distinct worlds, the one he left behind and the one he was sitting in now. If he was not such a practical soul, he would probably be reflecting on the meaning of life.

Time to go. Malcolm came down to earth and took the elevator up to the eighth floor. He found the office he was looking for, knocked, and entered. It was a small open-plan space with six desks. An Asian woman rose from her seat and approached him.

"Good morning. I am Gemma Soriano. You must be Malcolm. Pleased to meet you. We are happy that you have time to help out. Let's go to one of the meeting cubicles where we can talk without disturbing my colleagues." They entered a small cubicle with a phone and just enough room for a small round table and three chairs. "We refer to these as telephone booths. Since the renovation and the open plan, these rooms provide a place for confidential meetings and where one can talk without disturbing colleagues. Please take a seat."

Gemma proceeded to explain her encounter with Nyala Beyene at the Hill Town Hotel in Addis and the subsequent meeting with Thabisa. She related how she needed to leave Addis precipitously due to a suspected case of food poisoning. On return, a brief investigation by the Audit Division could not ascertain any irregularities and the investigation was suspended, at least until the full audit of UNSFIS in two years' time.

"Then last week," Gemma continued, "the corruption hotline got a message from a journalist in Geneva who claimed that his, now estranged, wife had stolen some money from the UN. This might have warranted a low key and local investigation by the Inspector General at the United Nations Office of Geneva. When I discovered that the alleged perpetrator, a certain Alejandra Castillo, works at the International Computing Centre on UNSFIS related activities, some little alarm bells rang. It may be nothing at all, but if there is a link between Thabisa and Alejandra, this may amount to a conspiracy, and deserves further investigation. That's when we approached DPKO for a secondee with investigation experience. You come highly recommended."

"Thanks for the vote of confidence. It seems like an interesting challenge. I assume that you would like a rather discreet investigation, at least initially."

"Indeed, I would not wish food poisoning on anyone," Gemma offered, with a smile, by way of confirmation.

They chatted a little more and arranged for Malcolm to meet Katya in Audit and one of the Finance Officers in the Division of Administration and Finance who could brief Malcolm on UNSFIS. Malcolm spent two days at his desk reviewing some files, while waiting for the UN travel office to arrange a ticket to Geneva. After three days he was on the overnight Swiss flight LX23 from JFK to Geneva Cointrin.

Nicknamed the UN Shuttle, there were always many UN officials and delegates taking this flight. It would be particularly full at this time, during the Annual Session of the General Assembly, with delegates and officials returning from New York after the agenda items with which they were concerned were completed. Malcolm, relatively new to the UN, was possibly not aware that the precursor shuttle, Swissair 111, precisely that same month in September 1998 crashed over the Atlantic, as a result of an in-flight fire, with 229 lives lost. Nine UN Staff from WHO, UNHCR, UNICEF, FAO and WIPO were amongst the dead. Still in shock, the UN introduced a rule that the number of UN staff on a single flight should be limited – a rule that could never be policed as there was no single centralised booking agency.

Malcolm had a rather uncomfortable flight. Since the length of the flight did not entitle him to a business class seat according to UN rules, he sat in economy. He was a tall man, and his knees were barely short of the seat in front of him. To his relief, he was not sitting next to a talker and he tried, mostly unsuccessfully, to get some sleep on the overnight trans-Atlantic flight. He took a taxi to his hotel, conveniently walking distance from the Place des Nations.

Malcolm wondered what he could achieve in the few days he had available. He had few leads and just one prearranged meeting. After a croissant and espresso at a local café, he walked to the Palais de Nations. He had not visited Geneva before and was impressed with the number of UN buildings he passed along the boulevard to the Place des Nations. Before him was the grand avenue of flags leading up to the Palais. A security pass awaited him at the gate, and he was directed to Door 6 where the press offices were situated. There, a guard directed him to the offices of the Latin American press agencies, which he found without trouble, knocked and entered. There were several desks, but only one person already in the office. It was still before dawn in Latin America and in any case the conferences taking place at the Palais only started at 10 o'clock.

He had noted from the display board on the way in that the ILO Annual Conference was taking place and a few other smaller meetings – an UNCTAD commodity working group on trade in iron and steel, UNHCR consultations on durable solutions for refugees in Africa, WIPO, with Cornell and INSEAD, on deciding on the annual ranking for the Global Innovation Index (GII), a WMO working group on the Severe Weather Forecasting Programme (SWFP), and several others. Another busy talk fest at the UN.

As Malcolm entered, Gabriel rose from his seat and introduced himself. "You must be Malcolm Malouf. I have been expecting you. Thanks for coming so early. I wanted to talk to you before my colleagues arrive. Let's go to the press bar and chat before it gets too crowded."

Malcolm followed Gabriel past a souvenir kiosk, the sales counter of the UN Postal Administration, the UBS Bank and a travel agency and entered the Bar de la Presse. It was a cosy place, with Art Deco fittings and *faux* stained-glass windows in Aubrey Beardsley style along one wall, where, no doubt, later in the day journalists would exchange opinions fuelled by cups of coffee. At this early hour, it was quiet with only one other table occupied. They ordered a coffee and croissant, Malcolm's second for the morning, and quite possibly,

Gabriel's second as well.

Finding a spot in a quiet corner of the café, Gabriel started. "I must say I am consumed with guilt. Both my conscience and my impulsiveness probably got the better of me. Part of me regrets having contacted your office. On the other hand, I am surprised and pleased that you have taken my concerns seriously enough to come from New York to investigate."

Malcolm, as an experienced investigator, just let Gabriel continue with his monologue, without any interruptions.

"We had a happy marriage, Alejandra and I. Life was good to us. We both had excellent jobs and were very much in love. Somehow, I wish she had not confided in me. I am not sure if I would have been happier if she was having an affair. I might have lived with that if it was a fleeting indiscretion, but this took me by surprise and was a little too much. Maybe I am more sensitive to these matters, but I cannot abide dishonesty, if that is indeed the case. She claims it was just a small indiscretion, but where does one draw the line? I am sorry if it is a storm in a teacup. Now I feel I have overreacted and am wasting your time. My marriage is in tatters and it may be over what transpires to be a trivial matter."

Gabriel was finally silent. He took a sip of his coffee and played with the crumbs of the croissant on his plate.

"Do not be too harsh on yourself, Gabriel. Our job is to investigate these kinds of complaints." Malcolm knew they would not have necessarily followed up had it not been for the suspicions arising from that incident with Gemma in Addis. Of course, no direct link was established between Alejandra and Thabisa, except that they both were somehow linked to UNSFIS, a tenuous link at that. Malcolm did not fill the silence for a while but eventually jolted Gabriel from his introspection. "Tell me about Alejandra."

"She was...is, a warm and jovial person. Vivacious and fun to be around. She is self-confident and probably has a certain sense of entitlement. She comes from a very wealthy family in

Mexico and never wanted for anything. I am not sure where the family wealth comes from, but I cannot vouch for its legitimacy and prefer not to know. She got a good education in Mexico and at the MIT in Cambridge. She is very clever, there is no doubt about that. Whether she has a criminal mind, I am not sure. However, she could equally use her brilliance for unscrupulous endeavours, as much as for virtuous ones, if she was so inclined. Alejandra is good at her work, and from what I understand well respected and liked at the International Computing Centre."

"What did she actually tell you that prompted you to call us?"

"When I suspected her of having an affair and confronted her on that, she was at first very defensive, but then mentioned that she had stolen some money from the UN through one of the computer applications. She said that it was just an intellectual experiment to see what was feasible, and it was just a small amount and she had stopped."

"Do you know what computer application she was referring to?"

"No, sorry, no idea."

"Tell me something about her work at the UNICC."

"Frankly, I don't know very much. As you know, the UNICC supports UN agencies and some other international organisations with computing services. I do know that Alejandra works in a section which deals with Enterprise Resource Planning and application hosting, whatever that means."

Malcolm knew exactly what that meant. UNSFIS was an ERP application. "Does Alejandra travel a lot for work?"

"Not much at all. Most communication with clients is done remotely. She seems to be constantly in e-conferences on Zoom, Skype or Teams, sometimes to my annoyance as they take place at all hours in the evenings. She often got very agitated when I interrupted her when she was working at home. In the last two years she has been twice, I think, to the UNICC offices in Brindisi and Valencia. Oh, and once she went to Turin for a week to a management training programme at the UN Staff College."

"Thanks Gabriel. That helps a lot. Thank you for contacting us. It sometimes takes a lot of courage to do so. I can assure you our investigation will remain discreet and if I do talk to Alejandra there will be no indication that you contacted us or that we talked."

Gabriel and Malcolm parted ways. Malcolm found a quiet place to work in one of the empty conference rooms. He sent an email to the UN Staff College and asked urgently for a list of participants at the management training which Alejandra had attended. He confirmed easily from the UNICC website that the Economic Commission for Africa in Addis was a partner agency of the UNICC. Thirdly he made an appointment, for that afternoon, with the chief of the UNICC Platform Services Section. He was not yet sure as to the prudency of confronting Alejandra directly, although, after Gabriel's description of her, he was somewhat curious and eager to meet her face to face.

Until the afternoon meeting, Malcolm was relatively free, so he walked to the delegates' duty-free shop and bought some Swiss chocolate and then exited the UN grounds and spent an hour or two at the Red Cross Museum across the road, from which he exited more depressed than when he entered, but much wiser. He ate lunch in the ICRC museum cafeteria and then caught a bus up to the airport and walked the short distance to the UNICC Headquarters.

The Chief of Platform Services, Abidugun Abimbola (call me Abi) had a smile which stretched from ear to ear and greeted Malcolm like a long-lost friend. He offered tea and made Malcolm feel very much at home on a comfortable sofa in his spacious office.

"How can I help you, Mr Malouf?"

"Please call me Malcolm. As I told you on the phone, I am from the Office of Internal Oversight in New York. This is really a very preliminary investigation and what I am about to say should obviously remain confidential. Furthermore, until the investigation comes to a conclusion, the person we are investigating should not be discriminated against in any way, should be assumed to have done nothing improper, and should be treated normally."

Abi sat up straight and leaned forward as though a major secret was about to be revealed.

"You have a staff member, Alejandra Castillo, whom I understand from all accounts is an excellent worker. I am afraid I cannot share with you the accusations against her. What you can help me with is to describe Ms Castillo's work ethic and integrity."

"Well, this is indeed intriguing. I am surprised she has attracted the attention of the Office of Internal Oversight. As far as I am concerned, she is a gem, a real asset to the section. Alejandra is a diligent worker and demonstrates a great deal of initiative. What's more, she is a pleasure to look at, if you know what I mean?"

Malcolm chose to ignore that last highly inappropriate remark. "Abi, do you think that she could behave unethically, dishonestly, or inappropriately?"

"No, I cannot imagine it. She strikes me as an honest person."

"Thank you. You have been helpful. Oh, one more question. I believe Ms Castillo went on a management training to Turin early last year. Who selected her for this training?"

"I did. We were offered one place for the training and I saw in Alejandra considerable management potential. She was thrilled with the prospect and was grateful for my confidence in her. I like to reward good staff."

"Thanks Abi, I appreciate your help. May I reiterate that you should not mention to Ms Castillo that we had this conversation."

"My pleasure. I am sure your trip to Geneva was unnecessary."

Malcolm left Mr Abimbola's office with a dilemma. Should he confront Alejandra or find other avenues to proceed with his investigation?

Malcolm returned to his hotel and sat in the bar with a cold beer. He opened his laptop and skimmed his email. One from the Staff College. Attached was a list of participants at the leadership training about which he had inquired. There it was. Thabisa Maseko, Economic Commission for Africa, Addis Ababa, was also at the same workshop. Now this could not be a coincidence. Surely not.

Conspiracy

Meanwhile, in Versonnex, disaster had struck. Egon, well before his full life expectancy, was hit by a car on one of the small country roads near the Treasurer's house. Egon died instantly. The car did not stop, yet life for the Treasurer did. Egon, together with his grandchildren were the central focus of the Treasurer's existence. He no longer found purpose in going for regular walks and watched a great deal of television, even though he was fully aware that what he was watching had no intellectual merit. He still ate his daily croissant and the combination of calories in, and no exercise out, began to affect the size of his belly.

Kyros tried to be as neighbourly as a good neighbour should, but noticed that his friend was becoming increasingly depressed. He suggested that his neighbour get another dog, but this was met with "Egon is irreplaceable". Something needed to be done to prevent his neighbour vegetating.

A few weeks had passed, and after returning from work, Kyros went next door.

"This cannot go on," he said. "I will not leave this house unless you come with me for a walk."

"Thank you for your concern but I am not in the mood."

Kyros plonked himself in an armchair in the lounge. "Suit yourself, but I am not going anywhere. It seems we have an impasse."

"Kyros, you have your work and many years ahead of you, while my life is in the home stretch."

"You have no idea. My work is shit. I know I'm not respected at work. I just turn up and don't deserve the rather generous salary that I get at the end of the month. Frankly I should retire. In a few years I will reach 50. I am under graded and have no prospects for advancement. I might struggle to get a new job, but why care? Our little scheme has generated several million dollars. That should supplement my pension."

Kyros smiled.

The Treasurer was not sure whether Kyros was deliberately deflecting trauma upon himself as a ploy, or whether this confession was spontaneous. Whatever the case, it seemed to work. The Treasurer took pity on Kyros, but had no soothing words to offer.

"Indeed," Kyros continued, "I think we should agree to make my pension supplement more substantial. I see no impediment to the two of us simply siphoning off all the earnings. It would be quite a nest egg split two ways instead of five. What do you think?"

The Treasurer was somewhat taken aback with this suggestion. "Well, I did not expect this from you." Although he thought that actually this was true to character. It made him feel uncomfortable, as tempting as it initially seemed.

"I tell you what. Let's go for a walk, get some fresh air. It's a lovely evening. We will chat about the weather, the upcoming French elections, great places to go on holiday, your children and grandchildren and anything except money. I will give you time to mull over my proposal and we will revisit it at a later date. How does that sound?"

The Treasurer acquiesced and actually enjoyed the walk and the company. The elephant in the room – the walk without Egon – was ever-present but not mentioned by either.

Eventually, some days later, the Treasurer succumbed. Not to Kyros's urgings that they embezzle the embezzled riches, but to the realisation that if he was to survive to a reasonable life expectancy, he needed to find a new Egon. The Treasurer located a breeder of German Shepherds in nearby Givrins, in Switzerland, and within two weeks had bought a puppy, which changed his life. The Treasurer called the puppy Gustav in recognition of the fact that Gustav Klimt was the mentor of Egon Schiele and, in any case, he looked like a Gustav. He spent many hours walking Gustav and training him to heel, sit, shake, catch, and cuddle.

The Treasurer became his old self. He rarely reached for the television remote, yet he still enjoyed his morning croissant, and his visits to his grandchildren every weekend cheered him up immensely.

Kyros, on the other hand, was not happy. He had counted on the Treasurer's unhappiness to redirect his attention to thievery. Kyros felt that a thief of a thief was somehow honourable. He was, of course, fooling himself, but Kyros had never been one for intellectual honesty nor genuine self-awareness. All ideas of early retirement seemed to be set aside. He just did not want to give his boss the satisfaction.

Transgression

In all honesty, I am about to speculate here. You may believe that I have already done so during the telling of this story so far. You may correctly say that I couldn't possibly enter the minds of the characters. And you would be totally justified in thinking so. But, I do know enough about human desires to make some assumptions. I might be wrong, but bear with me and decide for yourself.

Malcolm was intrigued. He could not get Alejandra out of his mind. His curiosity got the better of him. It was not good practice to confront a suspect face to face until more evidence was available. He would not admit to himself that his curiosity resided between his legs as much as between his ears. He was stepping on taboo ground, he knew it.

The next morning, he went to Alejandra's office unannounced. Was she surprised when he introduced himself? Impossible to tell. She was either totally innocent or a bloody good actor.

Alejandra came around from behind her desk and sat opposite Malcolm. She crossed her legs. He averted his gaze to her eyes.

"How can I be of assistance, Mr Malouf?"

"Call me Malcolm. This is an informal chat and very much off the record."

"Do you always start your conversations like that?"

"I guess it's my training as a policeman."

"I have not encountered many policemen in my life. In Mexico they were to be avoided, not to be trusted. Can I trust you, Malcolm?"

She was a tease, and, as already suggested by others, had the most engaging smile.

Malcolm was not one for blushing, but he felt flushed and was sure his face was getting redder. The more he thought about it the redder he imagined he became. Alejandra was already gaining the upper hand, and what's more, seemed to be enjoying the encounter.

"I believe I am trustworthy, Alejandra." Malcolm did not even bother calling her by her surname. "The question is, are you?"

"Oh, I am totally confused. I thought you had come here to talk about one of my staff or one of my projects, not about me."

Clever deflection thought Malcolm. "No, actually, it is about you. May I ask, what is your involvement with UNSFIS?"

"Ah, the dreaded UNSFIS. A big mistake if you ask me. We, well 'they', created a monster. The UN is prone to do this from time to time. Then 'they' turned to us technicians to make it work."

Malcolm disliked air quotes, but Alexandra seemed to like animated speech.

"So, what is your role?"

"'Was' my role, more to the point." More air quotes. "I was peripherally involved in the customisation of the vanilla ERP system that the UN purchased. There was a lot of custom-isation required. Totally unnecessary in my view. The off-the-shelf product was already fit for purpose and quite robust."

"Were you at all involved with the banking module?"

"Thankfully no. I know little about banking. I can't even manage my own meagre income. Actually, I know little about finance generally. I was involved in the customisation of the procurement module, but I have no involvement with UNSFIS now, *gracias a Dios*."

Was that comment about her own financial management an unnecessary defence where no defence was yet required? Malcolm was not sure. Benefit of doubt for now.

"Are you a religious person, Alejandra?"

"Why? Oh, my reference to God. No, not at all, just force of habit. I grew up Catholic, but have well and truly lapsed. I do however consider myself a moral person. I do not need religion as a crutch."

Again, too much unsolicited information?

"Two years ago, you went to Turin on a management and leadership training. How was that?"

"The food was good. Sorry, I should be serious. I learned a few new techniques for better leadership. I am not sure that the costs justified the benefits. At the moment I only supervise two staff, so I would hardly call myself a leader. For sure I aspire one day to take on more responsibilities and I appreciate the fact that my supervisor supported my attendance."

"Did you by any chance meet a person called Thabisa?"

"I guess I must have. We were divided into many breakout groups and interacted with all participants. Do you know where she is assigned?"

Not a flinch. Malcolm could discern nothing from Alejandra's body language. "She is South African and assigned to the ECA in Addis."

"Ah, yes, I remember her now. A rather shy person, but pleasant from what I recall. We did not have an opportunity to interact much. Why do you ask?"

"Just curious, she seems to remember you quite well," he lied.

"That happens a lot I am afraid. I am gregarious and outspoken. I am not shy to ask questions or make comments in the training sessions. I'm not surprised that she remembers me."

Malcolm could believe it. "I think that is all for now, Alejandra. Thank you for your help."

"I am not sure I was much help. I don't suppose you will tell me what you suspect I have done wrong?"

"No, I am afraid I can't. This may go nowhere. Please do not talk to anyone else about our meeting."

"Understood. Malcolm, is this your first time in Geneva?"

"It is."

"In that case may I ask you whether I can offer you some hospitality tonight. I could take you to a good Mexican restaurant, a rarity in Geneva, or maybe for a fondue?"

Malcolm should have said no. It is always inappropriate to fraternise socially with a person under investigation. "Thank you, that would be nice. No disrespect, but I can give Mexican a miss. There is no shortage in New York, but fondue sounds interesting."

"Excellent. I will book at the Auberge de Savièse on the Rue de Paquis. The restaurant is somewhat a Swiss cliché, but the fondue is reliable. Shall we meet there at eight?"

It was agreed. I won't bore you with what I imagine the conversation, nor the fondue was like. I can only assume that the conversation was light and the fondue heavy. Clearly Malcolm Malouf, the burly policeman from the poor western suburbs of Sydney and Alejandra Castillo Rivera, the very attractive Mexican from exclusive Lomas de Chapultepec, connected.

I say this deliberately, as Alejandra invited Malcolm back to her apartment for a margarita ("I can at least inject some Mexican character into our evening," she insisted). The margaritas – there were several – did their work, Alejandra's sensuality did its work also, and Malcolm took his inspection responsibilities beyond the acceptable. He spent a passionate night with Alejandra, the pleasure erasing any guilt until the taxi ride back to his hotel, in time to pack before taking another taxi to the airport to catch his plane.

Malcolm, as much as he tried to analyse Alejandra's motives, and his own indiscretions, could come to no firm conclusions, except that that one night was one of the highlights of his investigative career. Was she guilty? No idea. Was he going to recommend further investigation? He thought so. There was something of the devil in her and he did not want to let the investigation wane. Or maybe he just wanted to see her again.

End Game

It was now just short of three years since Alejandra, Thabisa, Hamiz, and Kyros met at the Staff College in Turin and soon after that started their "project". Their joint accounts were bulging. Kyros informed the other three that the Treasurer had informed him that there was the equivalent of $21,435,287.34 in the Genolier investment account as well as the two banks in Jersey and Bahamas. Additional ongoing deposits of $4 million had been made in Monero crypto-currency. The amounts in the banks did not accrue a great deal of interest, but over the three years one Monero XMR, the unit denomination, increased from $132 to $497. It remained vulnerable, and everything could potentially be lost, but the Monero value had increased by $8 million. Total: some $33 million divided by five. You do the math.

Through their encrypted communications with each other, they decided it was time to divide up the profits. Alejandra did not tell the others about her encounter with Malcolm, although she felt that it was too close for comfort. She not only wanted to take the profits but wanted to stop the scheme altogether.

Kyros was very much ready to see a dividend in his own personal account so that he could finally resign. However, he saw no reason to stop the scheme. He was a little upset with the Treasurer for not having agreed that they take it all, but if the embezzlement continued, he could, in any case, amass much more.

Thabisa was overcome with guilt and found it hard to sleep and was feeling increasingly less motivated at work. She would have given the money back if there was a way to do so, but she could not arrange to get Nyala's job back. Maybe she could deposit all or some of the money in Nyala's private account. That would be risky, as Nyala would easily put two and two together and realise she had been right about

Thabisa. Would Nyala keep quiet and keep the money or would she stand by her principles and seek revenge on Thabisa? Hard to tell. In any case Thabisa was also of the opinion that the scheme should stop and then she could think how to do good with the funds. She really would like to get a good night's sleep.

Hamiz was rather neutral. He was content in Cairo, although the Libya trip, and the misery he had observed there, still hung heavy in his mind. Also, he had slowly begun to realise that he had not been treating his family well. He had been an inadequate husband and father. Hamiz thought that taking the earnings and sharing them with his family might assuage his conscience for the way he had treated them. He was ready to follow the group consensus, but would certainly not have objected to closing shop, so to speak.

They concluded that, given each of their preferences they should stop the scheme and take their "earnings". Kyros was asked to consult the Treasurer on how they could each get a share. Clearly, they could not transfer the money to their regular personal bank accounts. They would have consider-able difficulty explaining the origin of the funds.

No problem. The Treasurer would simply open five offshore accounts under five new shell corporations and suggest that each open one or more accounts in different banks and each month deposit an amount equivalent to their salary. In that way the banks would not be suspicious. Major purchases should be avoided like yachts moored at Marbella or expensive and ostentatious cars, but purchasing a property or two on the Greek Islands or Bali or a chalet in the Swiss Alps, with a well-chosen estate agent or lawyer should not be a problem.

They agreed that they should take the next three weeks to open their new personal accounts while the Treasurer sorted out the five offshore accounts.

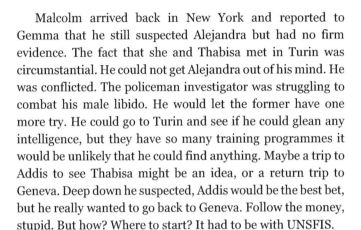

Malcolm arrived back in New York and reported to Gemma that he still suspected Alejandra but had no firm evidence. The fact that she and Thabisa met in Turin was circumstantial. He could not get Alejandra out of his mind. He was conflicted. The policeman investigator was struggling to combat his male libido. He would let the former have one more try. He could go to Turin and see if he could glean any intelligence, but they have so many training programmes it would be unlikely that he could find anything. Maybe a trip to Addis to see Thabisa might be an idea, or a return trip to Geneva. Deep down he suspected, Addis would be the best bet, but he really wanted to go back to Geneva. Follow the money, stupid. But how? Where to start? It had to be with UNSFIS.

Gemma told Malcolm that Katya in Audit had already tried, but saw no reason to dissuade him from looking a bit deeper. She introduced him to Katya and, after briefing him, she introduced Malcolm to the Chief of Financial Management in the New York Secretariat who in turn offered to assign a finance clerk to work with him for a week.

Nguyen Hanh Minh had only been in the UN for two years, but clearly, in Malcolm's opinion, had a bright future. She had entered the UN through a competitive exam. That is no small achievement as each year about 25,000 young people compete for some 90 positions. Hanh Minh was born in California. Her parents left Saigon by boat in 1981 and spent two years in the Galang Refugee Camp in the Philippines before being resettled in City Heights, San Diego. They stayed in California for 21 years and did quite well financially, having started a business selling kitchen and banquet supplies to hotels, restaurants and catering establishments, but they never quite accepted the discrimination they encountered in the United States. They felt Vietnamese first and American came a distant second. One day, when Hanh Minh was only eight years old, they packed up and left for central Vietnam, joining the growing number of return migrants. They had sufficient funds to open a 20-room hotel on the main street in Hoi An, with a restaurant serving "authentic" local food to tourists. The business performed very well.

When their daughter was 17 years old, they realised that she could get a better education in the United States as a private student, one of a growing number of "high net worth" Asians paying exorbitant fees to attend ivy league universities. Yes, money talks, but generally these students outperformed the majority of other students. Hanh Minh was no exception and after graduating from Stanford and working with one of the most prestigious accounting firms in Los Angeles, she applied for the UN Young Professionals Programme on a whim, and to her surprise, at the age of 23, found herself in New York.

Malcolm and Hanh Minh worked well together. He learned that her two names meant moral and intelligent, and she demonstrated a surfeit of both.

But where to start?

"I think Katya was correct in looking at the bank accounts," said Minh. "I looked already at the bank accounts in Addis and found no oddities. It took me a whole day to check the transactions for just three months this last year. It's not hard to believe there are so many transactions. Deposits are manageable, just a few hundred, but payables are just enormous. There are over 30 UN agencies in Ethiopia and just the salary payments run into the thousands. Thabisa's payments seem normal, and since she has payment authority over the Economic Commission for Africa programmes, I checked those and found nothing strange. In any case, the Chief of Finance needs to check and endorse all payment vouchers against supporting documentation."

"Wow. Thanks Minh. I have an idea. I understand that

Thabisa has regional oversight and access to the UNSFIS financial module in the Horn and East Africa. Can you look at the banks in the region and see if there are any anomalies?"

It took two days of laborious work. Djibouti, Eritrea, Somalia, Kenya, Uganda, Tanzania, Burundi, Rwanda, Sudan and South Sudan. The last of these took a short time as the banking system was rather rudimentary, but the others were slow going. In Sudan, Somalia and Eritrea she found some strange anomalies in the payments to the National Refugee Commissions. The funds coming in from UNHCR did not match the outgoings. She noted also that more Toyota Landcruisers were purchased each year than approved in the budgets. But that would require a country audit. She was amazed it had not been spotted. As she saw no link with Thabisa she sent a note to the Audit Division and moved on.

"There is only one curious thing," she told Malcolm after she had done as much as she could. "I checked all the bank codes in the system for all 10 countries against the International Bank Register and found that the Thika Commercial Bank, for which there is an UNSFIS code, does not exist. It was coded three years ago and there are no funds going in or out of the account. There are plenty of other banks in the system which are dormant, but this bank is a phantom bank, so to speak."

"Does Thabisa have authority to open bank accounts in the region?"

"I am sure she does. However, there are no funds passing through the account. It just hasn't been used. I need to give it some thought, but while rather odd, I cannot find anything wrong. Nevertheless, something is just not kosher." Malcolm smiled at how quickly Minh had become a New Yorker.

(Now, it will be recalled that the Four's embezzled cents and pennies did not pass through the bank account but were held in the UNSFIS transit account. While they were earmarked for the TCB, they were siphoned off before being actually deposited in the non-existent bank.)

Meanwhile, Malcolm contacted the Staff College in Turin again, and asked for a more detailed list of attendees at the management training: their function, location and the agencies for which they worked. He also asked for any photographs they had from the training. He gleaned very little. There was only one photo – the ubiquitous group photo taken in front of one of the training pavilions. They all looked happy and apparently satisfied with the prospect of becoming competent leaders and managers. Alejandra, looking glamorous as always, was not positioned next to Thabisa. The photo was taken a couple of days before the end of the training. Of course, they might have been astute enough, if they were indeed co-conspirators, not to be seen too much together. Either they were calculating or there was indeed no connection between them. It was impossible to glean much from the photo. There were five participants from Geneva. Were they connected in any way? There were also five from New York and the rest from a range of other duty stations. Amongst the 30 participants, 25 different UN agencies were represented.

Malcolm contacted the five New York based participants and interviewed each. Apart from all confirming they enjoyed the training, they could not remember whether any participants spent an inordinate amount of time with Thabisa ('rather shy but sweet') nor Alejandra ('very gregarious, talkative and vivacious'). The last of the three descriptors came from the two male participants and was a testimony to the poor impact of their gender sensitivity training. Another dead end.

Three days later, just before Malcolm was about to leave the office, Minh barged in without knocking (most unlike her), clearly very excited. "I might have found something. It might be a red herring, but it seems rather odd. Anomalies never sit well with a finance officer."

"Pray, tell."

"Remember the Thika Commercial Bank? I could not understand why there is a fake bank in the system and no funds entering or leaving that account. I looked a bit closer at the underlying coding and found that the TCB has a corresponding bank in Geneva, and that is a real bank, a bank that does indeed exist. It is a small private bank, one of many based in Geneva, which deals with high worth clients. It is called Banque Genolier. I tried to research them as best I could. It's not easy as they are most secretive; let us say, discreet. I did however check their list of publicly registered correspondent banks. The TCB was not amongst them. Indeed, they have no correspondent banks in the region. I guess they would use reputable global banks as intermediaries if required. It did not surprise me, however, that they do have correspondent banks in well-known offshore banking locations, although I only found that out by doing a random search and retro-checking banks in these locations. Banque Genolier appeared in some cases. Banque Genolier is the kind of bank that would keep its connections to banks in such locations confidential."

"So, Minh, if I understand you there is a tenuous connection between a phantom bank in Kenya with a private bank in Geneva?"

"Yes, very tenuous, but a connection nevertheless."

Under normal circumstances, Malcolm may not have followed that lead without a greater link, but they had no other leads and besides, he did not need too much of an excuse to return to Geneva.

Malcolm made a case to the relevant manager in the Investigation Division and the budget for a three-day mission to Geneva was approved. He took the overnight UN Shuttle from JFK to Geneva, the short train ride to Cornavin central railway station and walked across the tram tracks to the Hotel Cornavin. Why did he choose this hotel? Because Malcolm

129

was a fan of Tin Tin who, with Captain Haddock, visited the hotel in *The Calculus Affair* to warn Professor Calculus that he was in danger.

The first order of business was to call Alejandra.

"Hi, Alejandra, it's Malcolm from New York."

"Malcolm, I know where you're from. I recognise your voice. How are things in New York?"

"Actually, would you believe it, I'm in Geneva. I have an investigation at the WHO," he lied. "I would love to catch up while I'm here. Are you free for dinner tomorrow night?"

"What a lovely surprise." She assumed he had no such assignment at the WHO, which, if correct, was cause for concern. "Dinner would be great. There is a very popular restaurant just near where I live. I will book. It's called the Café du Soleil. Let's say we meet there at 7. Maybe we can then return to my place for a night cap?"

It was agreed. To Malcolm the night cap idea sounded good. He wondered whether he would be able to control his anticipation over dinner.

Alejandra had different thoughts. Time to urgently pull the plug. Alejandra sent a message to the others. "Looks like we are under investigation from New York. I have just been contacted by an investigator from OIOS in NY. I think we should wrap this up immediately. If you agree, Thabisa and I will shut down the siphoning from UNSFIS and while we cannot remove the Kenya Bank from the system, we can code it as dormant. I will tomorrow close the Banque Genolier account by transferring all funds to the Jersey account. I am afraid closing the account must be done in person. Kyros, please ask the Treasurer to sell the crypto, and transfer all funds equally to our respective personal offshore accounts. Please confirm." They all did, and the winding up of the scheme was put in motion. Alejandra felt relieved.

Explaining that she was only in Geneva for one day, Alejandra immediately made an appointment at Banque

Genolier for the next morning at 10:45 with the private client advisor, Monsieur Wallenberger. Probably around the same time, Malcolm rang Banque Genolier, explained his purpose and made an appointment with the bank manager, Monsieur Aristide Genolier III for 10:30.

The area fronting the central station was almost like the area around most central stations. The Paquis did boast some rather seedy hotels, where rooms were rented by the hour, but it was Geneva, Switzerland, so one felt all was controlled and safe. Malcolm bypassed Paquis and on crossing the Rhone at Place Bel Air he entered a very different world. Here the buildings were solid, square, old, established and usually anonymous. Any plaques on the doorways were discreet, usually brass or chrome, polished daily, to shine like the gold in the vaults below the streets where he walked. There were banks with familiar and unfamiliar names, but also companies with names that conveyed not an inkling of their purpose: Global Trading GmbH, Zifix S.A, Belowski Bros. Sarl, AtoZ Contracting PLC, and the like. Malcolm could only guess in what they traded and fantasised that he was a character in a novel delving into their secrets, penetrating these thick stone walls, uncovering their sordid business.

At 10:25 Malcolm entered the building housing Banque Genolier on the Boulevard du Théâtre and took the vintage caged elevator, complete with fold down bench, to the fourth floor, slid back the concertina gate and was presented with a rather ornate and very solid mahogany door. He rang the bell. The door was opened by a gentleman in an impeccable pin-striped suit who inquired as to Malcolm's business and asked him to wait in the reception area. Off the reception area, there was a long corridor flanked by offices to the left and to the right.

At precisely 10:30 Malcolm was escorted down to an office befitting a sixth-generation Swiss private banker. Aristide Genolier sat behind his massive desk, stood and welcomed

Malcolm in Oxbridge English, with a hint of that charming continental lilt. After shaking hands, Genolier retreated behind his desk again and Malcolm sat on one of the antique guest chairs.

"Welcome to Banque Genolier Mr Malouf. How may I be of service?"

"Thank you for seeing me, Monsieur Genolier. I am sure you are rather busy so I will not take up much of your time. As you have been no doubt informed, I am an investigator with the United Nations. There is a possibility that one of our staff is using this bank to launder United Nations money. This is a most serious matter and, as you can imagine, is of great concern to the Secretary-General who has insisted on a zero-tolerance policy. If I give you her name, could you give me any indication to the validity of our suspicions?"

"Mr Malouf, you are no doubt aware that I can not divulge such information about a client. Quite frankly I am surprised at your naivety. My sincere apologies for being so blunt, but I fear you are wasting your time and mine. All I can say is that we must adhere to certain statutory and regulatory guidelines, and it is highly unlikely that a bank of the standing of Banque Genolier would tolerate, or be party to, money laundering."

"Monsieur Genolier, you must accept my apologies. I would never suggest impropriety on your part; however, we fear that this staff member is using this bank to channel money from a bank in Kenya to offshore accounts."

"A bank in Kenya you say? This is highly unlikely as we have no correspondent banks in Kenya. Funds could only come from a reputable international correspondent bank with branches in Kenya and the source of funds would be scrutinised by them. I am afraid you have had a wasted trip Mr Malouf. My assistant will show you out."

Aristide Genolier did not hide his frustration. Malcolm was somewhat embarrassed, not totally surprised, but his fishing trip had achieved two things: an excuse to come to

Geneva and confirmation that Banque Genolier would not receive funds from the Thika Commercial Bank in Nairobi.

The dapper assistant appeared at the office door and led Malcolm down the corridor. Now that was strange. At the other end of the corridor Malcolm spotted a very well-dressed woman entering an office. It was just the most fleeting of glimpses, but he could have sworn it was Alejandra. Well, truth be told, he would not have sworn that under oath in a court of law, as she was decked out in a manner so sophisticated that it was not consistent with his image of Alejandra, an IT specialist at the United Nations. As he walked back towards the hotel, he could not get that image out of his mind. What kind of an investigator am I? he thought, and after one block, turned around and decided to wait unseen in a doorway of a building across the Boulevard. In any case, he had time and if it was not Alejandra, he could confirm his error and it would not hurt to get a better look at a high wealth beauty.

She exited the building rather soon after. Clearly a very speedy meeting, a short transaction. Malcolm was not sure whether he was disappointed, surprised, or angry with what he saw. Probably all the above. One thing for sure, what he saw, this transformed image, confirmed that she was one of the most stunning women he had ever seen. He could not wait for the rendezvous at the Café du Soleil.

Malcolm left the hotel at 6:30pm and took the trolley-bus up to Petit-Saconnex, arriving precisely at 7. Alejandra was already there, at a table in the courtyard under a very mature chestnut tree. It was a warm evening and she was wearing a 1950s floral dress, the kind his mother would have worn. For sure she wore it well. Not the sophisticated Alejandra who had business with Banque Genolier, but stunning beyond doubt. They greeted each other with a *bisou* on each cheek. Alejandra was warm and relaxed, Malcolm tried hard to convey the same. He was still conflicted as to whether to confront her or not about his morning undercover surveillance. He knew he probably should, but there were risks. Alejandra was a cool customer and probably would have found a convincing excuse. Also, he did not want to risk his amorous relationship with her. At least he would enjoy the dinner and conversation in that perfect setting.

And a very pleasant meal it was too. They had eaten fondue on their first encounter, so they opted for the standard *steak frites* with a green salad accompanied by that typical Swiss dressing – close to the French dressing but somehow asserting its own identity. They drank local red wine from the banks of the Rhone. The waiter, with the endorsement of Alejandra, recommended the chocolate mousse and espresso to follow. The conversation flowed easily. Not a mention of embezzlement and related matters. He asked how her day had been at the UNICC. "Rather uneventful. A fair bit of coding." She asked how his day had been at the WHO. "Not particularly exciting and rather inconclusive. I will need to go again tomorrow." They moved on to talk about non-work-related matters.

She renewed the invitation for a night cap and they walked the short distance to her apartment. She offered a Swiss eau-de-vie de prune, or two, which they enjoyed on the balcony with a view of the lake in the distance. The kiss came naturally as did their retirement to her bed. Alejandra lay naked face down while Malcolm made an amateurish attempt to massage her neck and back. The techniques may have been lacking, but his strong hands seemed to do the trick.

It just came out, involuntarily. "Alejandra, by chance I saw you today at Banque Genolier. I was on my way to look at the Opera House," he lied. "Do you have business with that bank?"

Quick as a flash, "I don't, but my father does. He does business with some trading companies in Zurich and Geneva and he banks at the Genolier. He sometimes asks me to represent him. I am not happy doing it, but one can't say no to papá." Alejandra thought: *Am I turning into my father with deception and lies?* Malcolm could not see her facial expression. He probably did not want to. He just wanted to believe the story.

Alejandra turned, pulled him towards her and kissed him passionately. Malcolm succumbed to what followed. *To whom am I making love? The young Mexican civil servant or the sophisticated chic woman I spied exiting the bank. I cannot shake, that magnificent image, still so vivid in my mind.*

Malcolm and Alejandra drank their morning coffee together before they parted. He would have liked to see her again before he left, but decided that he had already overstepped the mark, having a relationship with someone whom he was investigating. He realised that his judgement had been compromised. There was no point staying in Geneva any longer and he changed his flight for that day, checked out of the hotel and took a long walk along the quays of Lake Leman, enjoyed the spring weather and reflected on the case, struggling to separate his yearning for Alejandra and the few facts he had gleaned from his investigation.

The next morning as he entered his office, Minh rushed in. "While you were away, I had an idea. I checked the central bank holding account in the Nairobi UNSFIS. That's the account where income is held in transit before being paid into banks. I compared the total number of transactions each year for the last five years and over the last three years there was an unexplainable exponential increase. I am amazed that the system was not programmed to pick up such anomalies. Then I randomly chose single days over the last three years and I was flabbergasted. On some days there were thousands of transactions. Small amounts in, and small amounts out, and would you believe, they appeared to be directed to Banque Genolier. Look, I'll show you."

Minh opened the computer. "Let's go into the central bank holding account for yesterday. Look. Wait a minute, that's weird, just 56 movements. Let's look at last Tuesday. Aha, 700 transactions. There can be no reason for this unless the fraudsters have stopped the scheme."

"Can you trace the person who arranged the transactions?"

"Highly unlikely. The arrangement was probably set up more than three years ago. It's absolutely brilliant. Whoever did this is a genius. It's fully automated – seamless. It could be any staff member with access to the banking module in UNSFIS. That could be several hundred people. If it was a normal payment such as a purchase of goods, payment for services, installment to an NGO or salary payment, we could trace the relevant payment voucher and see who the action and approving officers were. In this case the amounts are minuscule and there is no voucher associated with the movements. I am afraid we have discovered, more or less, what happened, but not who did it. By the way, what did you discover at Banque Genolier in Geneva?"

"I am afraid it was a wasted trip. The bank manager was, as we might have expected, totally tight lipped, indeed angry at my impertinence. Apart from confirming that their bank has no correspondent banks in Kenya, I gleaned absolutely nothing. We may need to close the investigation. At least they have stopped. If you wish you can continue your work and see if you can recover the money, but my investigation is over and I shall complete my report as inconclusive, with no further action on the part of the Office of Internal Oversight.

Epilogue
On the Roost

Kyros, eager to look at his actual earnings, and having little to do all day, checked his offshore accounts on-line every half hour. At one point he realised he was going crazy logging in, the same repetitive clicks and passwords, all to no avail. He got up and went for a coffee on the 11th floor, and then down to check again. Nothing. He took a long lunch – actually he always took a long lunch – then went to his office to check. Nothing. By mid-afternoon, he went for a walk to the UN Diplomats shop at the Palais des Nations to buy some Nespresso capsules. That took 45 minutes. Came back, checked, nothing. The Treasurer said the transfers would be pretty much immediate. By the end of the day, Kyros was exasperated.

Kyros went home and before even entering his house went next door to see the Treasurer.

"I checked my offshore accounts today. There is nothing there."

The Treasurer looked dumbfounded. "That's most strange. I made the transfers the day before yesterday as we agreed, and given that it's a bank-to-bank transfer, the funds should certainly be there by now. Wait until tomorrow morning. I am sure the delay can be explained."

Kyros checked again before he went to bed, could not sleep, so checked at 2:00am. After all it was daytime in Jersey and Geneva, even though they were asleep in the Caribbean. Nothing. In the morning he sent an urgent message to Alejandra, Thabisa and Hamiz, and asked them to check. Also nothing.

Alejandra sent a message to Thabisa: "Can we trust Kyros? His concern may be a smokescreen, a misdirection. Maybe he is in league with the Treasurer. Maybe there is no Treasurer."

"There must be a Treasurer. Kyros is not bright enough to manage a deception like this on his own. To tell you the truth, Alejandra, I would be so pleased if the money did not arrive. I have had enough of this scheme. I want to go back to sleeping well at night."

Alejandra could empathise with Thabisa, and in some ways was sitting on the fence. She too, felt some guilt, not much, just some, after her deception with Malcolm whom she genuinely liked. Maybe it was time to turn the page. She had lost Gabriel through her indiscretions, and she did not want to lose Malcolm.

"Thabisa, I feel for you. Let's see what happens. If the money does not arrive, so be it. It's about time we got on with our lives, without the stress. That said, we make a good team. If ever you have a chance to come to Geneva, we will get together. I would like that."

"It's a deal. Stay well. We'll be in touch."

Now, you may wonder whether I had the intention to return the money from the outset. Did I get involved out of greed, or was it, as I told Kyros, out of boredom? I cannot remember when it occurred to me that I had no right to the money, or maybe I am just too ashamed to admit, to you, that it was rather late in the piece. I certainly have no need for the money, as tempting as it may be. After 33 years working in the UN and having reached the director level, I have a very handsome, inflation-adjusted, pension. My house in Versonnex was paid off years ago. My two children – one a banker, the other a hotel manager with the Swissôtel chain – are married with young children of their own. For them any inheritance from me would be superfluous, and, in any case, passing the money on to them would raise questions in their minds, not to mention with the Swiss or French tax authorities. So, you may quite rightly conclude, that there was no advantage, at my stage in life, to keeping the money and giving it back was the only logical option. An anonymous contribution of over 33 million dollars to UNHCR would, no doubt, have been well received. I imagined an intern in the Donor Relations Section wondering to whom to address the thank-you letter.

Disclaimer and Commentary on "When Your Chickens Come Home to Roost"

This is a work of fiction. The events depicted here are not real and all the characters are fictional. As much as my former colleagues might like to think "I know who that is", they (you) are wrong. No character is modelled on a real person, including myself. UNSFIS is my own creation, although the concept is close to reality. That being said, much of the context, the UN agencies and the description of the locations are all fairly accurate.

The United Nations comprises organs in which the member states play a defining role. These include the Security Council with five permanent member states which have veto powers and 15 temporary rotating member states drawn from different regions. The General Assembly comprises all 193 member states and territories of the United Nations, each of which has one vote. A subsidiary organ of the General Assembly is the Economic and Social Council (ECOSOC) on which all member states sit, and they have a governance role over some UN agencies.

In a different category are what are known as the programmes, funds and specialised agencies of the United Nations as well as departments of the UN Secretariat which is headquartered in New York. These include such agencies as UNDP, UNICEF, UNHCR, FAO, WFP, the International Court of Justice, the World Bank and many more – some 80 entities in all. These are all expected to be apolitical. There are the humanitarian agencies, the development agencies, agencies that support other agencies, economic affairs agencies and those specialising in technical standards and norms. Some are operational or field oriented while others have no or minimal representation in field offices. Some report to ECOSOC and some report to an executive committee comprising member states. Sometimes politics rears its head in these executive committees, but it should not, in principle, influence the neutrality of the agencies' work. These agencies have their headquarters in New York, Geneva, Vienna, Nairobi, Rome, and other cities worldwide like Montreal, London, Copenhagen, Addis Ababa, Washington and others.

Thus, while the Security Council, the General Assembly (and to some extent the Human Rights Council which is an intergovernmental body and not to be confused with the Office of the High Commissioner for Human Rights) are political, the agencies are expected to be apolitical. Of the latter, there is no doubt that some are more effective than others, yet most do good work.

Yes, there are flaws in the United Nations, but it is important when praising it or criticising it not to lump all organs and entities together. It is a truism that if the United Nations did not exist it would need to be created, and while there is much room and need for reform, in today's world any new creation would probably be inferior to what we have now.

There have been cases of fraud, serious mismanagement and sexual abuse in the United Nations, of that there is no doubt, but most staff are honest, dedicated and hard working. The negative press certainly taints the UN's reputation, but this needs to be juxtaposed with the considerable good work that the UN accomplishes.

I struggled long and hard to decide whether a story like this would reinforce negative misconceptions about the UN. That is the last thing I would want. The dedicated staff and the good works of the UN should not be negated by the odd bad apple. I wrote this story, because I like to read (and write) a good story. That is all this is, a story, and it is up to you to judge how good it is. The UN was good to me, and, in a modest way, I hope I contributed positively to its objectives.

For those readers who have worked with the United

Nations, much in this story, and dare I say, personalities, may be familiar. Where you find inaccuracies, the fault, whether due to my particular perception, my choice to alter some facts to help the narrative, or my lack of knowledge, is certainly mine. For those who are not familiar with the internal workings of the UN agencies, I hope this will give you new insight into an unfamiliar environment. But, please keep in mind, that the plot is pure fiction.

Water to Dust

July 1988 and October 2022

Could it have been avoided? Probably. Hindsight is the source of much regret. Of course he should have known better. That's what everyone who knew him, and even those who didn't, commented in hushed tones, not wanting to cast aspersions, while acknowledging that they too may have acted just as recklessly. After all, he was not a stranger to these kinds of conditions.

Alistaire Fitzroy Abercromby-Calthorpe, known to his acquaintances simply as Fitz, had travelled that road before, from Luuq to Mogadishu. But that was at a different time, when the dictator ruled and the land was at peace. When the dictator ruled and the land was at peace? That was something Fitz had always found difficult to reconcile. Did the ends justify the means? Ask the journalists, opposition leaders, outspoken dissidents, even just the simple shopkeepers who let slip a negative comment in a bar, and all the others languishing in the overcrowded Somali jails. Yet the streets were calm, petty crime was low and most people just accepted that status quo. They knew that the dictator was corrupt. It was not a big secret that he, and his clan, owned most of the pineapple and banana plantations from Afgoye down the coast as far as far as Kismaayo, where the Shebelle and the Juba rivers converged and flowed into the Indian Ocean.

Fitz had always been fascinated by these aquatic veins of life, yet the cause of such rivalry between the clans and between herders and planters. By the time the rivers entered Somalia from the highlands of Ethiopia, they were, at times, no more than a trickle. When they did flood, if the seasonal rains came with the regularity that they once did, the plains would transform into muddy lakes, crops would be washed away, and the riverine villages submerged. Curiously the floods could frequently be more devastating than the droughts, and life was hard.

The camel and cattle herders followed the weather and at any convenient place for grazing along the route, lowered their *aqals* from their camels, and the women erected the stick frames over which they threw their woven mats. That was temporary home, until the land became too barren for the livestock or it was time to pass by one of the market towns. Fitz had always found that the dignity of these transients matched the majesty of their camels. Both were survivors, although times were changing and with scarcity came conflict. It was no longer safe to roam the lands between the Shebelle and the Juba. Many had fled to safer lands, if these could be found. Others simply survived or perished along with their camels and cattle.

Since his first visit to Somalia to cover the floods in Luuq and Dollo, where the Juba formed the border between Somalia and Ethiopia, Fitz had covered the conflicts in Rwanda, Sudan, Bosnia, Afghanistan, Iraq and Yemen, but for some reason he had always been drawn to Somalia. He found it hard to believe it was 40 years since he was just a rookie reporter in Somalia. Maybe, because it was his first foreign assignment, Fitz had a special, probably romanticised, affection for the place. He respected the generosity of the Somalis, in spite of their frequent aggressiveness towards each other. He had seen it elsewhere: in Thailand, Burma, Yemen, Iraq. How could such gentle, kind people be so monstrous and brutal, and acquiesce to the autocracy of dictators and tyrants?

Fitz acknowledged that he pursued drama, death and destruction for every story. Conflict, misery and hardship sold newspapers. He had seen more refugees on the roads he travelled than most, and sadly had to admit that he was now so numbed by these encounters that it was an effort to keep seeing them as individuals, as people, rather than numbers. But, as a good journalist, he knew the value of a human-interest story. "This is Fatima, a single mother with three small children. She fled her village after a raid by the Lords Resistance Army. I asked Fatima..." The stories, in essence, were the same, always the same. It never ended, and this was how he made a living. Was he a parasite, a news junkie, or a valuable messenger? Fitz not infrequently mused whether he was indeed a catalyst for change in his own small way, or whether he should have embraced a career in politics, law, finance or property development like his father, uncles and brothers.

On that first trip, Fitz flew into Addis and hitched a lift on a UN Beechcraft all the way to Dollo. As the single engine circled to land, he could already see the extent of the flooding. Villages were submerged, the conical tips of the thatched roofs peeking above the water level as if gasping for breath. Bloated cattle, goats and sheep, floated on the surface. The regular landing strip at Dollo was submerged so they landed some kilometres west, on a makeshift dirt strip on some higher land. The pilot circled low and traversed the strip just 10 metres above, before attempting a landing, to announce his arrival, to check the condition of the ground and to scare a few animals off the runway. Makeshift shelters had sprung up, adjacent to the strip, on this relatively high plateau above the flooded lands, not more than a few metres below. If the rains continued in the Ethiopian highlands, it would not be long before this parcel too would submerge.

Fitz wrote a few stories, replete with hyperbole, using words like "exceptional", "tragic" and "unimaginable" – words which he knew would have little resonance for his readers. He had yet to master the art, or is it skill, to write a story which moves the reader and truly reflects the images he witnessed. His editors would be happy but, for him, that was not enough.

There were no spare seats on the Beechcraft for the return to Addis, so he crossed into Somalia by boat – the Dollo bridge was submerged – hitched a lift the short distance to Luuq and, for the price of a small contribution to the MSF health clinic, managed to negotiate a ride with one of their vehicles to Mogadishu. They left at sunrise the next day, entering the outskirts of Mogadishu just as the sun was about to set over the Indian Ocean. In this light the whitewashed structures conveyed a golden and welcoming glow. They had stopped in Baidoa, at a roadside shack, for a plate of goat and rice. They drank Coca Cola, and instant coffee served with tinned sweetened condensed milk from mismatching chipped cups, the brown stain inside the cups, a testimony to years of use.

They passed police checkpoints along the way and the driver paid a 'toll' each time. At the last checkpoint, at Afgoi, the police seemed not content with a few shillings from the driver, calculating that the three white faces in the passenger seats might be more lucrative. They asked for identification papers and travel permits. Fitz handed over his passport and press card together with a few shillings. Clearly not sufficient. He had no travel permit. It was only then that he realised he had entered Somalia illegally and had no right to be there at all. Fitz refused to pay more *baksheesh* – he had principles after all. The standoff became increasingly uncomfortable. Someone needed to break the stalemate.

Fitz looked in his bag and retrieved a personal letter from his father, Sir Reginald Abercromby-Calthorpe. Dictated in stilted, formal language, it was, as always, typed by his father's secretary on personalised stationery, purchased from Smythson's of Bond Street, ostentatiously adorned with the letterhead and crest of the House of Calthorpe. "Dear Alistaire," it read, "Although you are aware of my disapproval of your gallivanting around the world, a foolishness which is frankly hard to understand, I trust you remain safe. Whenever you come to your senses, you know there are more appropriate professional opportunities in England consistent with the Abercromby-Calthorpe name..." et cetera et cetera and signed, "Your father, Reginald Abercromby-Calthorpe." Fitz handed the letter to the policeman, who perused it carefully, pretending to read English. The policeman returned the letter with a smile and a nod, and having saved face, allowed them to proceed.

The discomfort of the drive was compensated for by the beauty of the landscape, alternating desert and lush valleys. The Juba, and when they reached it by late afternoon, the Shebelle, were flowing fast and had brought the normally dormant desert alive. If it were not for his aching body from the long journey in the back seat of a Landcruiser, Fitz would have been in very high spirits indeed.

Fitz found a room at the Juba Hotel. The hotel had seen better days, but he was too tired to find an alternative. He checked under the bed for cockroaches, not that he could do much about it, and took a shower, the head of which sprayed the cold water in all directions but down. He awoke to the sound of the *muezzin*'s call to prayer and ate a decent breakfast on the restaurant's terrace overlooking the sea, observing the early morning fishermen carry their catch up the beach to a cluster of sarcophagus-like concrete slabs which served as the fish market. The next day he flew to Nairobi on Somali Airlines with his memories, an affection for the landscape, and desire to one day return.

That day did come, 34 years later. This would likely be his last assignment, Somalia providing the bookends to his journalistic career. Fitz was feeling his age. He was tired; had seen too much misery. He had said that before each recent assignment, but this time he convinced himself it was for real. This would be the last.

In Somalia, time had moved on. The dictator was gone and the storm after the calm had been calamitous. Leaving the airport, he could see rubble wherever he looked, the scarred evidence of years of internal strife. There was an uneasy peace, punctuated by car bombs in Mogadishu and rebel attacks and kidnappings in the provinces. But Fitz was not here to cover the politics, that was yesterday's news. Drought was today's news.

The next morning he joined a charter flight up to Luuq, together with six other journalists, all of whom he knew from the circuit. These reporters gathered at the same watering holes, in the so-called 'war hotels', in Sarajevo, Goma, Kandahar, Sanaa and Juba. Truth be known, their stories were often simply fabricated over a beer in the bars in such places, pieced together from hearsay and shared snippets. Fitz looked at these colleagues and wondered what the collective noun for a group of journalists might be: a pod, a brood, a gang, a swarm? Fitz liked the imagery of a 'swarm', but settled on a 'pen' of journalists, finding the ambiguity amusingly appropriate.

No problem this time finding a dry landing strip. The whole upper Juba valley was one huge landing strip – caked dry after three years without a drop of rain. Beside the strip stood the *Rubb* Halls, the huge white warehouse tents managed by the World Food Programme, and beyond, the sad, makeshift shelters of the displaced, drawn to the food and the services provided. His colleagues took two hours to look about, take pictures, jot down notes and interview the givers

154

and receivers. Then they boarded the plane back to the Croce del Sud Hotel in Mogadishu, one of the few hotels still standing and the only one that sold beer. Mission accomplished. The stories could be filed the next day; the drought was not going away in a hurry.

Fitz, having found a driver willing to drive him back to Mogadishu, on the same road he had taken all those years before, ignored the urgings of his colleagues to jump back on the plane. They called him reckless, a fool, but he had an urge to explore a bit more, to reminisce. This time he walked across the dry riverbed under the Dollo bridge rather than crossing in a boat above it, the impact of nature measured in metres. He wanted time to reflect on his career and tot up the balance sheet. The next day Fitz would finalise his last despatch.

They left Luuq the next morning, early. The road skirted what was once a river for some kilometres and then they turned east to cross the inter-riverine basin, now very much a misnomer, towards the equally dry Shebelle. The gravel road was in disrepair – rutted and uncomfortable – so the driver left the road, choosing the soft, dusty soil off-*piste* amongst the parched acacias. They were not the first to do so. There was a maze of tracks sometimes parallel, sometimes criss-crossing, always confusing.

Engulfed in this wilderness, as the forks approached, Fitz would play a mind game to pass the time. Would the driver choose the left fork or the right? He noticed that the driver did not always take the track with the deepest rut, the track most taken. It was all very random.

Fitz asked the driver how he knew which track to take. "Experience", he replied, which begged the question of what logic the driver used the first time he drove this route. Fitz did not bother to ask. The Landcruiser slid in the sand, jolted in the ruts and swerved to avoid a rock or a dry acacia bush, leaving a wall of dust behind. The driver was adept.

Sixty-seven forks in one hour. A fork every 500 metres or

so. 33 kilometres. Two hours and a half had passed. Just 84 kilometres, give or take. He could have looked across at the dashboard and come to a similar conclusion, but this was as good as any distraction to pass the time. As a young boy, he recalled the drive every summer with his parents to their country estate in the Lake District. He and his brother, Antony, played mind games then too: spot the animal in the clouds; find a number plate from London; and I Spy. Then he would say, "Are we there yet?" He knew it was a standing joke, but it was tradition.

"How much more of this terrain?" he asked the driver.

"Not much more," was the totally unhelpful reply. So, he kept choosing forks. After all, there were no clouds, no other vehicles and the driver was not likely to play I Spy.

They stopped in Buur Hakaba for lunch (goat and rice, Coca Cola and instant coffee with sweetened condensed milk) in the shadow of an impressive monolith. His memories of Buur Hakaba were of a lush agricultural zone with a flourishing market. So much had changed. The acacias and grasslands had turned to brown and the livestock, the few remaining, had turned to skin and bone. The goat on his plate had little meat.

From Buur Hakaba they took the so-called road. It was no better than the off-road option, but it was, he was told, safer. Fitz considered counting potholes, but they were too numerous, so he dozed off as best he could, opening his eyes suddenly whenever they hit a pothole that caused a jolt larger than the others, or when the car swerved abruptly to avoid them. It might have been after one hour, or perhaps two, that Fitz was awoken by the gunshot. The windscreen was shattered and Fitz was in no doubt that the driver next to him was dead. Fitz had observed danger and violence many times in his career, but this was the first time that he was, or was about to become, a victim. Fitz, himself, was now "the story".

Fitz sat still, he raised his hands above his head, as he was trained to do, and tried to remain calm. There were five gunmen – well, not all were men, three of them must have been no more than 14 years old. Four surrounded the vehicle, assault rifles menacingly aimed at him, while the fifth manned the machine gun on the pick-up tray of the *technical*. All were chewing Khat. Drinking and driving is not a good idea, but chewing a stimulant drug while wielding a weapon is, in all likelihood, more precarious, especially when the weapon is aimed in your direction by an adolescent. The driver was unceremoniously dumped on the ground and the Landcruiser abducted along with Fitz, who was invited to lie face down on the tray of the *technical*.

When Fitz did not arrive at the Croce del Sud that evening and was not to be seen the next morning, his colleagues alerted the British Embassy. The next day the ambassador received a ransom note with a four-million-pound price tag. A week later, the Prime Minister said in a press conference, "We do not negotiate with terrorists, but we are praying for him," knowing full well that the Moslem God and the Christian God were not really on the best of terms and indeed may not have communicated with each other for some time. From his seat in the House of Lords, Antony Abercromby-Calthorpe made an impassioned plea for his younger brother's release. No mention was made of paying the ransom, although the Abercromby-Calthorpes would have considered four million small change. The *Times* and the *Guardian* prepared obituaries to Alistair Fitzroy Abercromby-Calthorpe who "lived on the edge and faced danger at every turn to bring his stories to the general public". Into the obituary they wove words like "exceptional", "tragic" and "unimaginable". Then they filed it away, waiting for the opportunity to go to press.

Trying to Make Sense of it all

May 1990

Shit, is that the time? I hate this last-minute rush. I should have just hung out at home and gone to the meeting from there. Why the government didn't give us an office on the Island is a mystery. I guess beggars can't be choosers.

Sten grabbed his bag and walked the shoddy corridors to the lift. The building vibrated as a large truck passed through the middle of the carpark, at the third-floor level. *This place should never have had offices above a highway. Only in Hong Kong.* The lift descended and Sten walked the block to the Yau Ma Tei MTR. Just four stops and he arrived in Central. A dash across Statue Square. *No Filipinas – it's not Sunday.* After taking the shortcut through the lobby of the HSBC building, he dodged the Queens Road traffic and darted up the Battery Path steps two at a time, reaching the Central Government Offices pretty much in record time.

Sergeant Lee only gave his pass a cursory glance. Having followed the same routine twice a week – Mondays and Thursdays – for the last eight months Lee recognised Sten. He nodded. Lee remained passive, maintaining a formality becoming of his gatekeeper role, and a deference dictated by the assumption that Sten must be somewhat important to be

159

invited to the meeting. Sten was not wearing a uniform, so deference to rank was not possible. Since he was probably 25 years younger than Lee, deference to age was equally unlikely. But, he was attending, so respectful formality was due.

There was a lift, at which others were waiting, so Sten took the stairway option, down the three flights to the sub-basement, entered and took his seat near the end of the table, way down in the pecking order. He always felt somewhat uncomfortable. He was, after all, somewhat an imposter; not totally sure of his role in the meeting and never knowing the limits of his interventions. All the others belonged. Sten was an outsider, a visitor, indeed, more akin to an observer. They were all nice to him. Well, at least they tried. The British amongst them were easier to read, but it was harder to discern the true attitude behind the Chinese smiles.

Sten surveyed the room, scanning those present around the long boardroom table. No need to count – usually the same number of participants, mostly the same faces in the same seats. They knew each other well, in a formal kind of way. The average age was 50 years. Sten had just turned 30.

The windowless room accentuated the glare of the neon lighting. The wallpaper consisted of a montage of maps, charts and satellite images. A bank of clocks showed local time, London time, Washington time and GMT. It had the stereotypical look of a war room, designated as an Operations Room, referred to as "The Bunker". *I wonder whether it has ever served as a war room. Possibly in the Pacific War. Maybe this is where they now planned for 1997, which is just a mere seven years away and it is a forward-looking room.* But for now, every Monday and Thursday at 10:00 hours it was a very punctual present room. There was always a sense of urgency and, above all, an expectation of efficiency and professionalism.

Yes, there was some small talk as the participants settled into their seats. No one arrived late, at least not without a good reason; the uniformed amongst them out of habit, the civil servants out of respect. The whole city ran on time, so why should this be any different? The last to enter was the Refugee Coordinator, who took his seat at the head of the table. No messing about. Ralph Clifton was actually lots of fun over a glass of beer in the bars of Lan Kwai Fong, but as a representative of the Governor and the First Secretary, Ralph played his role well. As he sat the room hushed, the same effect as when a conductor raises his baton.

I like Clifton. Very British. Probably Oxbridge. Or maybe even a comprehensive schoolboy who worked his way up through the civil service. Less likely, but he has that drive. He does not give the impression of being entitled. He is certainly efficient, competent. I hear he has the Governor's ear.

"Good morning, ladies and gentlemen," (there was only one lady, apart from the note taker), "let us begin. Mr Fong?"

"Thank you, Mr Clifton. Since last Thursday I must report the arrival of 14 boats with an average of 114 persons on board. Among the total of 1,601 there are 312 families consisting of 505 males, 418 females and 678 children. As far as we can ascertain at the moment, there are 22 unaccompanied minors amongst the children. Most are Vietnamese, but there are some Lao. All have been registered at our Green Island Immigration Centre and are being transferred to the ferries."

That's a pretty large number. Up from last week again. I don't like Fong. It's typical of immigration officers. They see their job as keeping people out rather than helping them in. I guess it's a mindset. This magnitude of irregular arrivals would challenge any immigration department. I guess he's under a lot of pressure and just doing his job.

"Warden Choi," Clifton interjected, "as I recall the ferries were reaching their full capacity. Where do we stand?"

"There are five ferries at the Wanchai moorings. With these new arrivals, they have now reached their capacity. We might be able to find about 100 spare places at Whitehead and

Chi Ma Wan, but those facilities are already overcrowded."

Choi always uses the euphemism 'facility'. If a spade were a spade, then 'detention centre' would be more fitting. They come up with the most amazing options to cope with the new arrivals. Retired Star Ferries. Wooden benches for beds, buckets behind curtains for latrines. I cried. I cannot believe I cried, well maybe I can. I don't like Choi either, although it is important to remain civil. In all likelihood he does not like me. I am probably prejudiced, as he is portly, no, fat. Look at him. That cheesy grin. Lumbering and slow. I wonder what Clifton thinks of him. Up to his standards of efficiency? The Correctional Services Department are trained to run prisons and that's how they run the detention centres. It annoys me that they refer to them as "facilities". "That which we call a rose..." A poor choice of quotation, as there is nothing 'so sweet' as I can never get used to the smell.

"Chief Superintendent Wilson, any capacity at High Island?"

"None whatsoever. We are already over capacity and the Department of Water Resources have given notice that they want the reservoir back. They cannot divert the water for long."

The police, who run the detention centre at the High Island Reservoir, are actually more humane than the Correctional Services Department. I like Wilson. The police were always reluctant to run a camp, but the CSD were stretched. Sometimes I wish the Royal Hong Kong Police would manage more camps. Ironically they have a more humane approach.

"Ms Liu, can you provide any more ferries?"

Bloody hell, I hope she says no.

"I am afraid not. Already the Secretary of Transport is not happy. The lead in the *South China Morning Post* last week about the rat infestation on the ferries was not particularly welcome. We have since fumigated and I think the infestation is under control, but we need to phase them out, not add more. We have over 1,500 people, amongst them many children, sleeping on hard benches. The food boxes provided twice a day are inadequate and the sanitary conditions unacceptable. This is no way to treat human beings."

The men in the room felt uncomfortable. Most were looking down; Choi was doodling on his pad. Fong, who took the bait, in part due to his anti-immigration stance, but probably more so because he was a chauvinist, broke a brief, but awkward, silence.

"Mr Chairman, this is no place for such an outburst. We are all doing what we can under difficult circumstances. Each government department needs to pull its weight."

I bet Fong has never been on the ferries. In fact he has probably not been to any of the detention centres, just his immigration processing centre on Green Island. It's not the same. Indeed, I suspect he does not want to go, in case it falls below the threshold of even his low level of morality. I wonder whether he would cry? Hell, I can't believe I cried. I have seen squalor in Somalia, Kenya, Bangladesh, but never was I affected so much as on those shitty ferries. When it rains, there is no shelter. The sides are open to the elements. The tourists love it when they cross the harbour on the Star Ferry, a nine-minute crossing, viewing the iconic Hong Kong skyline. The outlook from a hard bench in the heat, wind and rain is of little consequence whatever the view, yet Fong belittles the opinion of the one person in the room willing to speak her mind and show some humanity.

Clifton intervened. "I take your point, Ms Liu. I can understand your frustration. We need to find an alternative."

Now was that genuine empathy, or one of those "I hear you but don't really care, it's beyond my control" type comments that so easily roll off the tongue? I know Ralph well enough to think it was probably genuine. He's a good bugger under that official English façade. He's certainly caught between that proverbial rock and hard place. The

Colonial Government tries to present a humanitarian face, but the Chinese have made it clear the camps must all be closed by the time the Union Jack is lowered. It was not a request, it was a threat. If the conditions are harsh now, what will happen to the remaining refugees after 1997? Here we are, with arrivals of two thousand a week and the Voluntary Repatriation Programme is reducing this number by only about 300 a week.

Whoa, what have I missed? I should pay attention. What's that guy saying? I've never seen him in the meetings before. We've had Navy and Army and a couple of spooks in suits, but I think this guy is Air Force. Where the hell is Shek Kong?

Clifton saw some confused faces around the room. "Flight Lieutenant Compton-Smith. Could you explain the location of RAF Shek Kong for those who don't know and explain what you have in mind?"

I'm sure most of them know the location of Shek Kong. Maybe this is for my benefit. It's pretty clear that Clifton has prearranged Compton-Smith's presence and knows what is to follow. Compton-Smith. Pretty sure he went to Eton or Harrow. He has wings on his uniform. This one is not a bureaucrat.

"As many of you know, RAF Shek Kong is a military airfield in the heart of the New Territories. It's about 30 kilometres from here as the helicopter flies. The runway is concrete with a grass verge along either side. It has a length of 1,905 metres. We are prepared to hand over, temporarily of course, half the runway. That means it would no longer be viable for fixed wing aircraft but 660 Squadron could still operate its Westland Scout Helicopters. Our preliminary assessment is that we could house up to 9,000 refugees in tents. We have 10-person tents in stock, but I think we can accommodate 20 persons in each tent."

Shit, that's 450 tents on a steamy concrete runway. Imagine the heat generated by all that concrete. Maybe the ferries are good after all. It's amazing the creativity (not a great choice of words) of these guys. They are really scrambling for new options. After the ferries, this one certainly takes the cake.

"Excellent. When can you receive the first refugees?" Clifton asked.

"Well, Sir, we have the tents, mattresses, blankets and manpower to set up billets for 1,000 new arrivals every three days. We would need the help of CSD to set up the kitchens and feeding facilities and provide utensils."

"Mr Choi, can that be done?"

"If you give us the authority, yes. We have some extra kitchen and serving units that we had held in reserve for Whitehead."

Authority, a euphemism for funding. I must say these guys are efficient.

"What about security?" said a Chinese man in a suit who mostly observed and intervened only infrequently.

Surely, they don't have a presence already?

"The perimeter fence is already in place. We just need to build a new one across the middle of the runway. I estimate that would take two days to construct. The army engineers are in place already."

Well, that confirms it. This is pre-cooked. A fait accompli.

"What about latrines?" Ms Liu again. Predictably.

"We cannot build sewage pipes. It would be too complex and costly. We have come up with a novel design which we think might serve our purpose. We will sink six 20-foot containers into the concrete, two thirds underground, side by side along the perimeter fence and place another container atop each. Steps will go up to the upper container which will house toilet cubicles. The waste will be collected in the lower containers, which we will periodically clear with an extractor pump on a sewage truck which pulls up outside the fence." Compton-Smith gave a smug smile, conveying a pride in the ingenuity of British Armed Forces' engineering.

Indeed, very clever, but I wonder about privacy. And good luck when they get the runway back and need to extract the containers. Maybe they will leave them as a gift to the Chinese. A kind of 'shitty' welcome.

Sten smiled. Nobody noticed.

"Mr Carrington. Any comments?" Craig Carrington was the Colonial District Administrator of the Yuen Leung District. This was his turf. He was a career colonial servant. Born in Nyasaland, he officiated as the Union Jack was lowered in Northern Rhodesia and would no doubt be around to see the same in Hong Kong. Craig and Sten were good friends and met privately at each other's apartments on the back side of the Island. Sten considered Craig an ally in matters of principle, but still understood he had to toe the official line.

"I will meet with the District Board tomorrow and I am sure I can convince them. As long as security is assured, they should not object. I will liaise directly with the Flight Lieutenant."

This was the new consultative process in action. The current Governor had been trying to instil a semblance of democracy into the governance of the districts. A bit too late and too little, but a positive gesture, nevertheless.

Clifton looked at me. "Has UNHCR any comment before we adjourn?"

I wish he didn't ask. I can never work out whether he is putting me on the spot or whether he wants me to inject a humanitarian voice into the proceedings. Well, there is Ms Liu, but no one pays attention to her. They probably don't pay attention to me either. They will in any case do what they want. I am just window dressing, albeit with an occasional voice, and maybe not so pretty. But I am here for a reason. Mr Conscience. I need to do my job.

"Mr Olsen?"

"Ah yes. Thank you, Mr Clifton. I think colleagues *(I like to refer to them as colleagues to establish an equivalence)* around this table are well aware that most facilities in Hong Kong do not measure up to the recognised international standards for asylum seekers. *(I see that Choi's and Fong's eyes have already glazed over. Choi has picked up a document, reading it, blatantly ignoring me.)* 9,000 persons on an area I estimate to be certainly no more than 30,000 square metres implies just over three square metres per person. This falls somewhat short of the acceptable individual living space per person and considerably short of the overall collective space required for a facility of this kind. The risks related to personal security and safety of the asylum seekers are considerable, not to mention problems of hygiene."

I could go on about refugee protection, access to water, the inadequate latrines, the lack of exercise space, the detention-like nature of the facility, but I would just create more annoyance for those around the table. I certainly did not want to jeopardise our guest status in the room.

"Thank you. We all appreciate your view and welcome UNHCR's input." *Patronising? Insincere?* "But this is Hong Kong, not Kenya. We simply don't have the land for your standards, nor do we have the luxury of time to plan as you, and indeed we, may like." *Remain composed.*

"I note that since we met last Thursday arrivals were 1,601. That presents an average of over 3,000 per week since early February. If the numbers continue, Shek Kong is but a short-term solution. Through you, Mr Olsen, I would like to remind the UNHCR Chief of Mission, through you, that if the Voluntary Departure Programme does not pick up pace, we will need to increase involuntary returns accordingly. We note your objections to that programme, but I think it must be clear to you that these stop-gap accommodation measures are not working."

Sten nodded, Craig gave him a consoling face, Choi and

Fong smiled, the others remained impassive.

"Any other business?" Choi raised his hand. "Mr Choi?"

"Thank you, Mr Chairman. I need to report that yesterday we had another incident at Whitehead. We were holding one of our information sessions with the resettlement countries. The consular official from the United States Embassy was speaking. The UNHCR Field Officer was present. As the American was explaining that the resettlement places from Whitehead were coming to an end and that it is in the best interests for the Vietnamese to return home, a young man got up and proceeded to stab himself with some sort of sharp object. The consular official started yelling at him to stop, that this display was unacceptable, and that acts of that nature will make no difference. Meanwhile my staff intervened and escorted the man to the clinic. There was a lot of blood, but the injuries turned out to be superficial. I believe that these sessions are getting the message across to most residents, but the hard-core gangs are being most disruptive."

"Thank you, Mr Choi. I think it best for now that single men are excluded from these information sessions."

Information, indeed. These are coercive sessions. However, I should not be so naïve. It may well be in the best interests for the asylum seekers to return, even if it is not totally voluntary. Blasphemy?

"I will meet again with UNHCR and the embassies and step up the sessions. I think that concludes our meeting. Next meeting 10:00am Thursday, at which time, Flight Lieutenant, I trust you can report that Shek Kong is ready for the first residents. Meeting adjourned."

Sten walked up the stairs with Craig. "God, you guys really are organised. I'm not sure how you manage it." *The least I can do is give credit where credit is due.* "But, I wish you could find your way to take a more humanitarian approach. At times it seems that we are talking about numbers, just digits, not human beings."

"Point taken, but you must see it from our perspective. You have your stance, which, by the way, many of us respect, but we have our constituents, a shortage of land, an increasing number of arrivals and no end in sight, except of course the handover in a few short years."

Sten had mixed feelings about the meetings. His presence was recognition of UNHCR's role, the humanitarian conscience, even if, at times, it was a thorn in the side of the government. Not that they cared. They took sovereignty very seriously. It trumped international obligations, to which lip service was possibly the maximum Sten could expect. On the other hand, he had a liking for his quasi fly-on-the-wall status. He could observe the workings of a well-oiled machine, even though some of that oil left a dirty stain on the Refugee Convention.

Before returning to the office, Sten stopped off for an espresso in the lobby café of the Prince's Building at Statue Square. He looked about. *Cartier to the left of me, Hermes to the right, here I am stuck in the middle...* The coffee was welcome. That tune, a favourite of his, playing in his mind, made him smile and, yes, reflect ...

> *"Trying to make sense of it all,*
> *But I can see it makes no sense at all.*
> *Clowns to the left of me, Jokers to the right,*
> *Here I am stuck in the middle..."*

Suitably caffeinated, somewhat depressed, and needing some fresh air, to the extent it was available in Hong Kong, Sten took the Star Ferry across the harbour to Kowloon and entered the Nathan Road flow. Flow was too kind a word. Deluge was better. *I'm sure that this road has more pedestrian traffic than any other in the world.*

He chose not to hurry back to the office. He cherished the time to unwind and, although dodging and jostling through Hong Kong's pedestrian arteries was not ideal, it seemed preferential to the administrative chores awaiting him in the office.

Sten then did something totally out of character. Crossing the Tin Hau Temple Park just behind the office, he saw one of the many fortune tellers who frequented the area crouched on the pavement. Sten sat on a bench and the fortune teller approached. Sten was not superstitious but thought that he would engage the fortune teller to help him economically. They cannot have a large income, but they were a Hong Kong institution and deserved support. At least that was a justification. He handed over 100 Hong Kong dollars and the fortune teller invited him to pick a card. The four of clubs, which was placed back in the pack and the pack shuffled. A small canary-like bird chose his card from the fanned pack. Sten feigned surprise. *The old sugar on one end of the card trick eh?* The fortune teller took a tatty brown notebook and turned to the four of clubs page and spoke in generalities: He said that Sten had a privileged life; that there were challenges ahead; that he would find both happiness and sadness around the corner; and he could look forward to a long trip.

"May I ask a question?"

The fortune teller nodded.

Ridiculous of course, but here goes. "What is the meaning of life?"

"Whatever you want it to be," came the reply as quick as a flash.

That Voice in my Head

June 1991

I can't tell right from wrong anymore. It was, I thought, harmless at the beginning, but now I think it had gotten a bit out of hand. The body was just the start, then the full-scale riot? Was I responsible? Probably. So possibly justice prevailed.

It was a confusing time. I had just arrived back in Erbil in late February, after the American bombing of Baghdad. The bombing in Baghdad was scary and I was relieved to be in a place of relative peace. It only lasted a month, but that was a month I choose to forget. My auntie and cousin were killed when a bomb hit their apartment building. We buried them in the night. There was no electricity, but we could see our way to the cemetery as the night sky was lit up with buildings on fire, tracer rockets and exploding bombs. We had no choice.

So, here I was in Erbil with my mother and sister. The Shiites in Basra started a rebellion, thinking that Saddam was weak after the Kuwait catastrophe. Then the Kurds decided – why not? – to start a rebellion in the north. Everyone thought the American no-fly zone would protect them, but the Americans let Saddam keep flying his helicopter gunships. What followed was a massacre. Thousands of Kurds were

171

slaughtered and hundreds of thousands fled to Turkey and Iran. At first Turkey closed the border but I think that the coalition governments pressured them into letting the Kurds cross. They did not stay long, just a couple of months. The coalition forces created a buffer zone in the north along the Turkish border. Saddam stopped fighting and Erbil became relatively peaceful yet still in government hands. The Kurds had de facto control over the mountains to the north and east of Erbil. It was a strange time in the north. In reality three separate chunks of Iraq were controlled by three separate entities. There were checkpoints everywhere.

It was six weeks ago that Mohammad approached me on the Qalat ring road below the entrance to the citadel.

"Hi, Amin. It's been a long time. What have you been up to since you left school?"

"Oh, Mohammad, it's you. Good to see you." That was disingenuous, and Mohammad probably knew it. I never did like the guy. He was a class bully and looked down on everyone. He was also a bit too orthodox for me. His father was an imam and his uncle owned about 20 shops in the grand Qaysari Bazaar, which he rented out to local shopkeepers. These included tinsmiths, candlemakers, stalls selling cloned cosmetics, clothing and textile merchants and gold and silversmiths. He had a monopoly on many of the spice shops, or if he did not own the shop, he was the trader supplying the spices. Mohammad was a product of riches and religion. Whereas I was a product of poverty and privation. My father was a tailor. I did go to the mosque from time to time, but I would not call myself a religious person.

I should point out from the outset that Mohammad and I were both Shiite Moslems, living in a country which was predominantly Sunni. It's hard to believe that we worship just one prophet, yet we still cannot get along. I guess the Catholics and Protestants have a similar divergence from their origins, but I can't recall that they ever came to blows. Oh, there is

Northern Ireland of course, so I guess all "love thy neighbour" religions tend to forget the teachings of the prophets from time to time. Separation of church and state? Phooey.

Anyway, back to my story. Ah yes, I was replying to Mohammad: "I spent a few years in Baghdad. I found a job with a cousin who owned one of those restaurants on the banks of the Tigris that roast fish splayed on sticks encircling an open fire. It was a good few years. The locals and tourists came in big numbers. I did not save much, but it was a living."

"When did you come back to Erbil?"

"After the calamity in Kuwait and the American bombing, the tourists left and my cousin could no longer keep me on. I stayed for a while during the bombing, but came back here in February. Since then, I have been out of work. I live with my mother and sister in Sarbasti. My father died from cancer a year ago. We could not afford the treatment." I wanted to change the subject. "What about you?" I asked him. "What have you been up to?"

"For a few years I worked with my uncle in the spice business and then I spent a couple of years in Iran, just across the border in Piranshah."

"What were you doing there?"

"You know. This and that."

Well, that's an unhelpful reply, I thought at the time, but I chose not to pursue it further, although I probably should have.

"Amin, I am part of a small group of like-minded friends. We meet socially from time to time in a small tea shop in the Qaysari. Actually, I'm on my way there now. Why don't you come?"

I should have heard the alarm bells ringing. Not only did I not consider Mohammad a genuine friend, but the "like-minded" comment is usually a euphemism for something sinister. He seemed to be fond of vagaries. It smelt of conspiracy. Maybe I was curious, or maybe I just wanted a cup of tea in the company of others.

"Sure, why not."

We dodged the heavy traffic on Qalat Road and entered the Qaysari through the passageway beside the Haji Abdul Qader Saeed Dabbagh Mosque. The sounds and smells accosted me upon entering the bazaar. The spices pungent, the honey sweet, the yoghurt a fermenting sourness, the clothing stalls musty and the tin furnaces smoky. The smells mingled with a familiarity, instilled since childhood. Mohammad navigated the alleys with a purpose, not stopping to check his route. This was clearly very familiar territory. I followed and was soon disoriented and lost in the maze.

We entered a tea shop with low ceilings and arched doorways. The walls were completely covered in a jumble of old photographs in cheap frames. There was no logic to their placement. It seemed as though they were organically positioned so that no empty space was visible, smaller photographs filling the gaps between the larger. Many were from last century, Erbil in 1900, the Citadel during its better days, a strange juxtaposition of a photo of Faisal II during his short-lived reign, next to a photo of Saddam's statue in Firdos Square. Other portraits depicted the current and previous owners' families – official posed photographs along with random snaps at family gatherings. And pictures of Ayatollah Khomeini and the Azadi Tower in Tehran. Regional history and geography randomly scattered on the walls. Photos for all seasons and reasons.

The teashop was crowded. All men. Supping tea with honey cakes and talking about business, politics, family and philosophy. In other words, dwelling on conflict and differences.

It came as no surprise to me that the current owner was Mohammad's uncle. The tea shop manager greeted Mohammad with a hug and a warm smile. Probably a cousin. Mohammad led me into a small side room. The "like-minded" friends had already arrived and were waiting.

We were five altogether. I recognised Nasir Farhat from our class at school. We nodded in recognition as though part of a conspiracy.

"Amin, I am sure you remember Nasir. This is Sajid Ghulam." It transpired that both were his cousins. And this is Berzan Ghaderi." I nodded. I deduced Berzan was a Kurd, the exception in the group. We were all about the same age and conversation flowed as easily as the tea along with sweet cakes. It was a seamless transition into politics.

"I hear the Governor has banned any form of protest in Erbil."

"That's not at all surprising. I am sure he gets his instructions from Baghdad."

"I saw that he sidelined Yasir Jaziri as his deputy and appointed a Sunni in his place. Since the war this place is a real mess, economically and politically."

"Prices have gone up considerably. It's due to shortages. Yesterday I paid 3 Dinar for a kilo of flour. Last year it was 1 Dinar. That war was a calamity."

"If you have dollars, you can get 11 Dinar to the dollar. The black market is flourishing, and the average Iraqi sees no benefit from the oil revenue."

"Regime change would be a good idea, but it seems unlikely. Look what they did to the Kurds. Massacred the shit out of them. Berzan you would know better than any of us."

Berzan sat in silence for a while. No one chose to break that silence. Nasir had touched a raw nerve. Berzan had fled with his family into Iran and recently returned. He hailed from Sulaymaniyah, but had come to Erbil in search of work, an objective which he found illusive. "My brother was killed at Penjwen, just eight kilometres before the border. We stayed in Iran for three months. Conditions were tough and last month we returned. It was almost worse back home. There was no food, our house was damaged from the fighting and we could not afford the repairs. That's when I decided to come to Erbil to find work, but I have had no luck so far. Mohammad, I don't know what I would have done if you had not befriended me last week."

It was so unlike Mohammad to make friends beyond family and sect. I still cannot figure it out. But I liked Berzan. He had a kind face and in spite of an underlying sadness, a charming smile. At least as a friend of Mohammad he might land some work.

The group was primed, and Mohammad got down to business. "We have a problem and we may be able to hit two birds with one stone, so to speak. Last night as the bazaar was closing, a young boy tried to rob one of my father's stalls. There was a scuffle. I am sure it was not intended, but the boy was stabbed in the scuffle. He bled profusely and died soon after. The police were nowhere to be seen and my father asked me this morning if I would dispose of the body."

I was shocked. Life seemed to have lost all value in Iraq. Dispose of the body? Mohammad could have been talking about a wilted flower or a rotten banana. Still, I sat in silence.

"I have an idea," Sajid said. "Why don't we dump the body on the steps of the Governor's office. That would certainly make a statement."

"Nice idea, but far too risky. Too much security and too exposed. We would be picked up in a flash." Nasir said.

I wondered what kind of "statement" it would make but that question just flashed in my mind and disappeared along with so many other unanswered questions. Nevertheless, I thought I needed to be seen to be an active group participant. I guess I had an urge to be relevant, so I offered, "I walked past there two days ago. Nasir is right. But, right next door to the Governor's office is a small house that was once a health clinic. I noticed a United Nations flag outside. Something to do with refugees. They have just one guard outside. There is a small lawn in front and a very low fence. We could drive right up to

176

the fence and throw the body over. It would be best if we were on the tray of a pick-up truck. We wouldn't even need to stop."

Mohammad looked at me with an approving smile. It appeared I had been won over, yet I still had mixed feelings. "Now that makes sense," he said. "I will get one of my father's pick-up trucks and we can do it this afternoon. I will drive. Amin, it was your idea, so you had better be on the tray. Who else?"

I had no way out of it now. I really got sucked into that one. Sajid volunteered to join me on the back of the truck. We all said our farewells and agreed to meet again in the same tearoom the next day. Sajid and I followed Mohammad to collect the truck and then the body. It was wrapped in a blood-stained shroud and was not very heavy. We drove the short distance to Salahaddin Boulevard. We passed the Governor's offices to our right, crossed the busy Sultan Muthafar intersection and Mohammad mounted the footpath passing close to the UN office. Sajid and I were ready and we chucked, oh what an undignified word, the body over the fence. Mohammad sped away from the city centre. I looked back to see a guard in a blue uniform shouting after the truck, but we were pretty much out of range to hear his cries.

Mohammad dropped me off at the edge of Sarbasti just a couple of minutes later and, in a daze, I walked the few blocks to my home. My mum asked how my day was. I replied that it was uneventful and went into my room, took my earphones and listened to western pop which I had taped off the *Voice of Youth* radio station. I turned the volume up, as loud as my cassette player could go, and lay on my bed thinking of Springsteen dancing in the dark and Bowie wondering if there was life on Mars. My mother would have been unhappy. "Why can't you listen to Kadim Al Sahir or Nazem Al-Ghazali and not that western nonsense," she would say. I just rolled my eyes and walked off. She meant well and she probably had a point. Iraq was changing by the day and we never knew what the next day would inflict upon us.

I was of two minds as to whether to return to the teashop for the next get-together with the "like-minded" but realised it would have appeared cowardly if I did not go.

When I arrived, a bit late, having got lost in the Qaysari maze, everyone was there. Nasir brought the morning paper. On an inside page there was an article with the headline "Dead body thrown into the UNHCR compound" followed by a statement from the police chief describing what happened with the ominous warning that "we are close to identifying the anarchist culprits". I had never been called an anarchist before. I guess it suited the government's political agenda.

"I am sure they have no idea who did it. We were out of there in a flash and I am pretty sure we were not identified." Sajid said.

I hoped he was right.

Mohammad's reaction was surprising. Rather than suggesting we lay low for a while he said, "As they say, 'movement is a blessing', action is better than inaction. We need to do something more dramatic. We need to protest or, better still, stage a riot."

"I don't see how we can do that," said Berzan. "There are only five of us. That's not much of a protest let alone a riot and we are sure to be arrested."

"I have given it some thought," Mohammad said. "What is it that people need most in Erbil?"

"Peace, money, housing?" suggested Nasir.

"All of those, yes. But one of the most immediate needs is food. How about if we put notices up in the market that next Tuesday the UN at their office on Salahaddin Boulevard will be distributing free food. Hundreds will turn up. We will have our crowd."

"OK, but then what?" Sajid asked.

"Then we step in. We provoke. We cajole. We agitate. We create a riot."

178

"You really think that will work?" Berzan said.

"I know it will work." Mohammad was confident about that.

It suddenly dawned on me what the "this and that" involved, when Mohammad was in Piranshah. He was very likely an *agent provocateur* at the bidding of Iran and his training was about to be put into practice. Now I was getting a little more concerned but kept quiet. There was momentum. Too late to apply the brakes.

And so it came to pass. Notices were prepared, notices were posted on shopfronts in the bazaar, notices were read, and on cue, crowds appeared. It started as a trickle, but soon all four lanes and the footpaths of Salahaddin Boulevard were blocked. Traffic backed up in all directions. You could see that the officials at the UN office were confused. People often approached them to claim asylum, but never in such numbers. The crowd was peaceful, that is until we arrived. We approached from the northwest. Our strategy was to have the crowd between us and the Governor's office. We walked through the crowd chanting, "Give us food! Give us food!" and the chanting spread like a virus.

With the predictability of the *shamal* winds from the northwest, the police and special forces, kitted out in full riot gear, moved in to disperse the crowds. We five were now spread out amongst masses and lost touch with each other. I can remember being amazed at the ability of just a handful of agitators to rile up a passive gathering.

Then the tear gas filled the air. Tears welled up in my eyes. I could not see well at all. With about 10 others I jumped the fence into the UNHCR compound. We expected to be chased away, but they let us into the building and gave us water to rinse our eyes. It did not help much immediately, but after about 15 minutes I began to see a little more clearly. By now the crowds outside had moved on, and also, it seemed, the Iraqi police and special forces. The UN staff were kind to us.

Apart from me, the others were innocent Iraqis who had just come to the office in search of food. Most were scared. All were disappointed.

We could detect that the UN staff were nervous about our presence in the office. I was not sure of their relationship with the authorities, and I began to be increasingly apprehensive as well. Through an interpreter, one of the UN staff asked that we follow him out the back door, across the small carpark to the lane behind the office. It was all going well until a pick-up truck with a machine gunner on the tray appeared. They must have been waiting. The gun was pointing directly at us. A few seconds and it could all be over. It was enough time to think back to my encounter with Mohammad just a week before. "Why don't you come?" "Sure, why not." One of those pivotal moments in one's life that can change its whole trajectory.

I don't know what got into that UN guy. Was he suicidal? Did he believe that good trumps evil? Did he feel invincible because the UN had standing in these parts? Did he feel that the UN armband he wore made him bulletproof? Me, I just thought he was an idiot, and wished it all to end quickly. He stepped forward and held out his arms in a gesture that was neither aggressive nor defensive. The standoff lasted just 15 seconds but seemed like the proverbial age. A shout from the cab. "Leave them," and they drove off. The angel, the idiot, stepped aside and we ran.

All the others ran down the lane towards the city centre. I just wanted to go home, so I turned left. The pick-up truck was not in sight, so I trudged slowly in search of composure. I was shaken and felt a considerable sense of guilt. What had this achieved? Probably just a clampdown on dissidence and certainly not regime change. As I walked trance-like down the road, I did not see the police van down a side lane. They emerged front and back. I had lost any will to run. I deserved to be arrested. I am not sure I deserved to be imprisoned. At the trial, the photograph of me on the back of the pick-up truck catapulting a boy's body seemed to clinch my fate.

Writing passes the time, although I am not sure that my story will ever reach any readers. Who knows?

Where in Hell is Walda?

April 1992

Of indeterminate age, yet probably over 60, old and weatherworn, Guya Goba Bule sat in the shade of his house, the mud so dry and wrinkled, not unlike his own skin, that it fell in lumps from the walls. Guya had no energy to repair the walls, although he knew it should be done. For that he needed water to mix with the soil, or even some still damp dung. He had neither. Guya had given up appealing to *Wok*, the god to whom all Borana appealed in troubled times like these. Four rainy seasons had come and gone, with nothing but a mere drop. The last of Guya's cattle, from which he derived both his status and livelihood had perished a month before, their dry carcases no longer giving off that horrid reek of death. He could no longer provide for his wives. All but five of his children had left for Nairobi; those remaining just waiting until they were of an age to do so.

Walda was now a shadow of itself. Once boasting 50 family enclosures, just a handful remained. Guya and his wives and children now survived off small amounts of dried meat, some milk from passing camel herders heading south in search of greener pastures, some wild ostrich meat, which was not to his taste, and some handouts from the people who came to

183

Walda from Nairobi.

Guya Goba Bule, feeling helpless, sat in the shade of his house and wondered why they bothered to come. The border crossers could have stopped in Moyale, but they said it was too close to the border so they continued on to where those white people, in their big white cars, had arrived and started handing out food. The border crossers probably had their own land, but they came to his. The white people came with tents and food. They came with drilling machines, looking in vain for water, so they brought water in big tanks on trucks and massive black rubber balloons to hold the water. The white people did not ask if they could use his grazing land. In any case it was no use to him now, and they had given him some food for his family.

Guya Goba Bule sat in the shade of his hut and every afternoon, between the time the sun was high in the sky and the time it set over the escarpment, he listened for the buzz of the plane, watched it pass no more than a few feet above his house and land on the small makeshift dirt strip next to the road. It took but a short time to disgorge its passengers, no more than can be counted on one hand plus a thumb. They unloaded some boxes, and then the plane took off to from wherever it had come. Today there were four men and a young lady. She looked around in awe and, it seemed to Guya, that she was uncertain what she was doing there. Two of those large white cars were waiting to whisk them to the camp just some 200 metres east. On their doors were blue signs, one had a little man between something that looked like hands and the other some corn and wheat held by a hand. Guya amused himself by looking at the blue signs. Many were different. They seemed to like blue.

The flight had been uncomfortable, and Varsha was apprehensive. She climbed uneasily down the steps, bringing her joints back to life after the cramped two-hour flight. Looking about she wondered whether it was a good idea to have agreed to this assignment. The landscape was barren and Walda village only consisted of a few mud houses. Some children ran out to watch and an old man sat in the shade of his hut and just observed the scene without emotion - dignified yet sad. Two Landcruisers pulled up closer to the plane, one UNHCR and one WFP. The drivers loaded the boxes and suitcases into the vehicles. Varsha and her new UNHCR colleague, Massimo, a community services officer, were taken to the UNHCR compound, while the others went presumably to the WFP compound. The drive was a mere five minutes at most. Tents with UNHCR logos stretched out in neat rows, left and right into the distance, either side of the road. Just ahead they approached a compound, almost indistinguishable from the camp itself, enclosed within a fence of dried thorn bushes piled no more than chest high. The makeshift gate of crisscrossed branches was dragged aside by a guard and the vehicles stopped in a small parking area just beyond the gate. UN and UNHCR flags hung listlessly from a pole next to the gate. There was not the slightest hint of a breeze, neither to display the logo on the flag nor provide a modicum of respite from the heat.

This was not at all what Varsha had imagined. Actually, she was not certain what she had expected but, without foreknowledge, had anticipated a compound more akin to her last assignment in Showak, where there was a reasonable town and where, in the securely fenced compound, prefab houses, kitted out with IKEA furniture, flush toilets and even air conditioners, were provided for UN staff. This compound was nothing like Showak. About 12 single-person safari tents were randomly scattered to the left. To the right, a large marquee, about 12 metres by 5 metres. Behind it, with her experienced eyes, she noticed two pit latrines and what appeared to be a makeshift shower surrounded by hessian sacking.

A young man approached with a smile as wide as a hotel manager welcoming a guest to a beach holiday in Cancun. "Good afternoon. My name is Declan. I'm the Head of Office and emergency response officer. Welcome to Walda." Varsha and Massimo introduced themselves. "We're so pleased you arrived. I must say that we've been pretty short-staffed, and you guys fill a few gaps. You must both be tired. Let me show you round, and to your luxury accommodation (his smile now transformed with a touch of sarcasm) and you can settle in. At six we all gather in the mess tent, the big one over there, for dinner, followed by our daily staff meeting. Follow me."

Varsha struggled a little to understand every word of Declan's strong Scottish accent yet smiled inwardly at the pleasant melodic tones. She reflected how it was not unusual for some colleagues, especially those who did not have English as their mother tongue, to struggle to understand her own accent. Declan was certainly very welcoming, albeit failing to hide what she detected to be some classic signs of exhaustion, possibly bordering on burnout.

As they walked to the accommodation, Declan explained, "You're both rather lucky. Last week the compound looked nothing like this. Since the camp opened we've been living in small single person camping tents, the sort you may take for an overnight hike in the mountains. We had a cook, who prepared food for us over a traditional charcoal fire. I'll not describe the condition of our latrine nor the makeshift shower we rigged up. Needless to say we all got pretty ill most of the time and it messed up our ability to set up the camp as effectively as we would have liked."

"Anyway, last week Branch Office Nairobi contracted a safari company to come in and set up something much better. Tourism has dropped in the game parks since that English woman was murdered at Masai Mara, and there are companies happy to cater for us instead of remaining idle. I actually think they like the change from their usual clients. I suspect we complain less. Ah, here we are. Varsha, this is your tent and Massimo you are in the next one. Not very soundproof, I'm afraid, but you have your own space and a wee touch of privacy. There are two pit latrines just yonder and a shower just beyond. Get settled and we'll gather in the mess tent at 6 when you can meet the rest of the clan."

Varsha crossed a small covered "veranda" with a director's chair under the shade of a canvas overhang, lifted the flap and discovered a camp bed with sheets and a blanket, a small side table and a metal chest with a padlock, presumably in which to keep her belongings. It was even possible to stand erect under the apex of the tent from where, hanging on a short wire, was a bare electric bulb. It was a yellow bulb, which she later learned did not attract mosquitos and other flying bugs, of which there was no shortage. Varsha unpacked her few belongings and ventured out to the latrine and shower.

Varsha counted the steps from her tent. Force of habit. About 20 metres. Acceptable. The emergency handbook stated that there should be one latrine for every 50 people in the emergency stage. I guess if equity and empathy with refugees was intended, two latrines for less than 20 staff would suffice. She was reminded of the slogan: "Walk in their shoes". Here, without choice, was the opportunity to do so. As far as pit latrines went this was state of the art, a proper plastic seat with cover placed on a wooden box base and the pit ventilated with a chimney. UNHCR blue plastic sheeting provided flimsy walls for barely enough privacy, but that could be easily improved with time. The shower was fed by a single hose of cold water, rather welcome in the heat. She could see ways to improve the drainage and would talk to whoever is in charge from the safari company. Get your own house in order first, she thought.

After a welcome rest on her camp bed, which was surprisingly comfortable, Varsha walked to the mess tent. She was greeted at the flap by a burley South African who looked and sounded like he would have been very much at home in apartheid South Africa. He towered over her by almost a metre and his girth was probably three times hers, but he had a welcoming smile, yet not the most refined choice of words.

"Ah, a new face. Welcome to camp bloody nowhere. Maartens, with two a's is my name. Nicolaas, with two a's, Maartens, but everyone just calls me Nico. You must be tired after a shitty flight and buggered in this heat, but you'll soon get settled. It's basic, but you should have seen the place before me and my guys got here last week."

Varsha, who was far from enamoured with the uncouth language, was almost ready to remark that they had done a shitty job on the latrines and showers but thought better of it. It was clear it would not be prudent to already antagonise Nicolaas with two a's. She smiled. "Nice to meet you Nico. My accommodation is very comfortable, thank you. I'm the new Water, Sanitation and Hygiene Officer.

"Well, I am sure the guys are happy to have you. Join your colleagues. Dinner will be served at 1830 hours."

There was a long table to the right. She was struck by the fact that it had a white tablecloth embellished with salt and pepper shakers and a couple of vases of, albeit dry, flowers. Clearly some adjustments needed to be made to re-purpose this camp from a safari camp.

There were seven persons around the table, all drinking Tusker's lager from the bottle. Declan rose. "Varsha, welcome again. We now have the whole team assembled. Let me introduce you. Everyone, this is Varsha Dravid. WASH Officer. Last post Showak, Eastern Sudan. Varsha, you've met Massimo, community services. Kofi from Ghana there is the protection officer. Ole, seconded from the Norwegian Refugee Council, is the genius who manages our comms. Check with him later and he will issue you with a handset. I guess your call sign will be Victor Delta. We'd be lost without Claudia over there from Argentina, assigned from the Emergency Standby Roster to take care of all admin matters and liaise with Nico the facilities manager, who I see you've had the pleasure of meeting. Finally, but super important, our two national field officers both from Nairobi, Mercy Njeri and Kennedy Otieno. Mercy and Kennedy work closely with WFP on food distribution, and with the NGOs on the distribution of non-food items. Varsha, I'll brief you more in detail tomorrow, but your main interlocutors will be UNICEF and OXFAM in the WASH sector, where there's much still to be done to reach acceptable standards. Well, that's introductions. I propose we relax until dinner is served. Varsha, a beer?"

The meal was beyond Varsha's expectations, although she should not have been surprised. This is what tourists in Masai Mara and Amboseli game reserves ate for dinner so why not at UNHCR Walda? She almost expected wild game meat but the chicken and vegetables, preceded by pumpkin soup and followed by banana fritters was most welcome after a long day. There was a side table with a hot water urn for instant coffee and English black tea, with what seemed like an endless supply of plain digestive biscuits. Varsha, in spite of her Indian origins craved an espresso or herbal teas, with maybe a higher class of confectionery.

The meeting was an informal affair. No real agenda, just a round table. Nevertheless, Varsha gleaned much from Declan and the team, who were all clearly good at their jobs. Most were recent arrivals. Declan and Ole were the veterans amongst them and had been in Walda a mere three weeks. But as the most recent arrival, from Varsha's perspective, all behaved as if they had been there for many weeks. Not at all surprising in a fast-moving emergency where the learning curve was steep.

Each in turn reported on their daily activities and raised the many challenges they faced. Walda refugee camp had been a reality for only six weeks and already had a population of 50,000, mainly Somalis and Ethiopians, a smattering of Sudanese and even a few West Africans and, apparently, some opportunistic Kenyans who were attracted by the humanitarian aid. An initial team was sent from Nairobi and as the influx was so fast, they improvised with registration. It was not clear to the current team, who had come up with the cockamamie ID card solution. They should have known better, but maybe they should not be blamed for their inexperience.

Declan asked Kofi, the refugee protection officer, who was responsible for registration, to explain the situation to Massimo and Varsha. Kofi produced two cards. "At the moment about 22,000 of the early arrivals have old ID cards. About 28,000 have these new approved plasticised registration cards. As you can see, the initial cards are primitive, and easily counterfeited." He passed the cards to Massimo and Varsha. Massimo looked; his mouth open with surprise. Varsha, turned old the card over in her hand and smiled, but realised quickly it was not a smiling matter.

5 weeks earlier

It didn't take long for the news to spread. Mengistu had fled to Harare and the government and army were in disarray. Tafesse Barentu didn't hang around. He discarded his uniform and took a bus south to Hawassa where his mother and sister still lived. They would struggle without his army pay, as meagre as it was, but his sister still worked in the coffee plantations. It would not be long before the famine bit harder and their lives would take a severe turn for the worse. But Tafesse had no option; in Addis he would be arrested for sure. Many of his comrades were already in prison and it was just a matter of time before he too would be snatched.

Tafesse remained in Hawassa for several months working in the plantations earning subsistence wages. How-ever, it was work and for a time he felt secure. And then he didn't. The factional fighting found its way to the Sidamo region and it was time to move on. He could not go north, back towards Addis, and Somalia to the east was equally in turmoil and unsafe. So Tafesse joined a seemingly unending wave of people going south. It was a five day walk through Kebado and Bule Hora with a shortcut through the Yabelo Wildlife Reserve down to the Kenyan border. He had a small backpack with some clothes, an old plastic water bottle, a few remaining shillings and not much else. The walk was hard, exposed to the relentless sun and constant risk of attack from hyenas of both the animal and the human kind. There was some safety in numbers, but the mixed feelings of urgency, danger and uncertainty played heavily on his spirit. Moyale, the border town could not come soon enough.

Moyale town straddled Ethiopia and Kenya, divided only by a small meandering dry stream bed. There was a large immigration and customs post straddling the main road, but the remainder of the border, flanked on both sides by a maze of dusty streets between houses, factories and workshops was essentially invisible. Crossing into Kenya was like crossing the road in any town to buy a chicken or an egg. Students, former soldiers like him and some civilians were fleeing the regime, the sectarian fighting and the famine, seeking refuge across the border.

Tafesse had now bonded with a small group of fellow Ethiopian travellers. They were told that it was still about a day's walk west to Walda. Before departing, they filled their water bottles in Moyale and bought some bread. The sun was low on the horizon when they set off, walking south to skirt the mountains and then west in the direction of Walda. They rested from time-to-time, walking through the night to avoid the heat. All of them were young and fit, except for a woman with two small children. In order to make progress during the cooler nighttime hours, they took turns carrying the youngest child on their backs. By eight in the morning they arrived in Sololo, the only village of any size on their route, and rested until late afternoon when the sun began to set, and then set off again for the five hour trek to Walda.

Around midnight they approached Walda where, even in the dark it was not difficult to find the camp. Rows of white tents were illuminated by the almost full moon. At the beginning of a "road" between the groups of tents they were approached by a Kenyan policeman and instructed to wait by a makeshift shelter until morning. They were no strangers to sleeping rough on the hard ground and were relieved to get some rest.

The sun rose quickly in the sky. Tafesse awoke to find that another 10 people had arrived while he was sleeping. Then a couple of other people turned up. They wore jeans and t-shirts but were distinguishable by their blue vests with UNHCR logos. They sat behind a table and the police officer helped form a line. The woman with the two children first, the single men after. One of the UN staff, a Kenyan, spoke English and there was an Amharic interpreter with him. The Kenyan opened a large register and noted down the details of each new arrival. Name, family member names if any, ages, nationality, town of origin. Each person received an ID card.

The card was simply an index card, one of those ubiquitous cards with a red line at the top and blue lines below. Each card had been cut in half and the name of the refugee written at the top. Below, a few details: "Tafesse Barentu, Ethiopian, Male, Single" The card was then stamped with a rubber stamp with United Nations High Commissioner for Refugees encircling the UNHCR logo.

The soldiers, students, and other civilians were separated and assigned a tent in three distinct but adjoining sections in the camp. For the students and soldiers, there were six to a tent. Each tent had an address written on a card nailed to the tent post. Tafesse was in Section B, Row 2, Tent 3.

Once settled, with their ration card, refugees went to a large warehouse tent and were given blankets, soap, sleeping mats, eating utensils, a mug and a plate. For single persons, cooking pot sets were shared. Names, along with the items they received, were recorded in a ledger.

Tafesse befriended a fellow former soldier, Garaakoo Waaqa who had just arrived in Walda two days before. There was not much to do in the camp; most sat around and chatted in small groups. Some played football in the dusty windswept open space between the Ethiopian and Somali sections of the camp. Once every week the refugees went to the ration distribution centre and were given their food rations.

With inevitable spontaneity, a small market was beginning to emerge on the road that dissected the camp. There was a barber, under his makeshift shelter with only a stool, one pair of almost blunt scissors, a comb and a shard of a mirror that was so small it served little purpose. A few vegetable stalls had sprung up and were a welcome addition to balance the standard rations of wheat flour, oil, and a few dried pulses. Tinned and dried foods were available from another shop and gas bottles with small single ring burners from yet another. There were a couple of tea shops and cafés with makeshift tables and stools. There was a stall, probably run by a Kenyan, who had a new Nokia 1011 cell phone. He sold minutes on the phone. Coverage was terrible but he did a good business allowing refugees to call home and say they were safe. Most refugees had never seen a mobile phone before. There was even a small informal post office. One local Kenyan sold paper, pens, envelopes and stamps and each week went by bus to the Marsabit post office, 150 kilometres south, to post the letters. Some money exchanged hands, but primarily food rations were bartered for goods and other services.

Tafesse and Garaakoo were sitting in one of the tea shops.

Garaakoo took out his ration card and gave it to Tafesse. "Tafesse, I have been thinking. This life we have now is not a life which I can endure for very long. The Meles Zenawi government does not look like it will go away and we cannot go back to Ethiopia. To sit around all day without any prospects is not what I had in mind for my life. What do you say we start a little venture?"

"What do you have in mind?"

"Look at this card. I think with very little effort we could go into the forgery business. I went into the little post office shop in the market. The guy there sells the same index cards. We just need scissors and a pen and we can make our own cards."

"What's wrong with the cards we have now?"

"I was thinking that we make new cards. If we say we have a wife and six children, we will get eight rations instead of one. We could open a stall in the market and sell the surplus."

"What about the UNHCR stamp? Where will you get that from?"

"We don't need it. Look again at the card I gave you."

"I see you have changed your name and have six children. Where did you get the stamp?"

"Look harder Tafesse."

Tafesse looked closer. It took him a while. It was not obvious at first glance and then it registered. The stamp was a mirror image of the UNHCR stamp. "How did you do this?

"Simple, just a little moisture and the image transfers. Let's make you a new card. Tomorrow we will go to the food distribution centre with the Ethiopian civilians and see if it works."

And, that's what Tafesse and Garaakoo did for three weeks. They had cleverly made wheelbarrows out of planks of wood and had fashioned wheels also from wood. The axle was a portion of tent pole. They were primitive, rather bumpy, but did the job to transport their now increased weekly ration which together amounted to much more wheat flour, pulses, oil and salt than one person can possibly manhandle.

Varsha immediately got down to work. She had had a sleepless first night. Although the bed was comfortable and she was tired, it was the snoring emanating from the next tent that kept her awake. Varsha's misfortune was having Nicolaas Maartens as a neighbour. He was equally vocal in his sleep as he was when awake. The croaking was so loud and ceaseless that she could well have been sharing her tent with him, heaven forbid.

Varsha took breakfast, buffet style, in the mess tent and greeted her colleagues who wandered in, chatted amicably, ate and went on their way. Everyone seemed to know what they had to do. Declan smiled as she came in and asked how she slept. "Fine," she said stoically, while spotting Nico over Declan's shoulder. Declan offered to take her to meet the WASH implementing partners, which she gladly accepted.

There was an organisation in the camp responsible for water supply and another for building latrines. Varsha met with the agency workers and discussed their plans. Water had to be trucked in and there were already some bladder tanks with banks of taps. It was insufficient and trucking very expensive, but there was no option. Drilling had so far been unsuccessful. Concrete paving was needed to avoid the muddy swamp that was forming around the water points. Many more latrines would be needed to get anywhere close to the required standard. The ratio of latrines to refugees was dismal.

It was an exhausting day, Varsha had surveyed the whole camp, identified the existing latrines and water points, and calculated roughly how many would be needed to make the camp habitable. She had her work cut out. They needed to a find a more reliable water source, and at the pace latrines were being built, they would have to resort in the meantime to using defecation fields.

After a nine-hour day in the searing heat, with only the briefest of lunch breaks, she took a cold shower. Initially the water coming from the hose, exposed to the sun, was scorching, but it soon became lukewarm. Before dinner, and before the sun set, Varsha, needing some "me time", sat in the director's chair on the porch of her tent and, most appropriately, started reading the recently published *Me: Stories of My Life* by Katharine Hepburn, which she had found in the Stanley Hotel bookshop, while passing through Nairobi.

The evening meal of beef stew, green beans and mashed potatoes followed by fruit salad from a tin, although rather tasty after a long day in the sun, reminded Varsha of the summer camp at which she volunteered after completing her Master's in Emergency Water Supply at Cranfield University.

During the after-dinner staff meeting, Varsha had an opportunity to report on water and sanitation issues, but felt the agencies were, as to be expected, doing a professional job given the numerous constraints.

"Trucking in water will continue to be a serious drain on resources. We need to get a second drill and look for ground water urgently. If we do find it, at least it will help the local population too." As she listened to the others, she realised that she was not unique in highlighting problems.

Massimo said, "The unaccompanied children are at risk of falling through the cracks. Also the death rate is so high that the supply of both adult and children's shrouds, which we use to monitor the death rate, are getting low. Their use in unanticipated numbers indicates that the rate is way above what it should be for even a newly established refugee camp. We urgently need to get more shrouds, but more importantly do something about the death rate. Clearly water, sanitation, hygiene, supplementary feeding and health care are all critical."

Mercy was concerned that "in spite of adequate stocks in the warehouse, some sections of the camp have not received their initial supply of non-food items."

Kennedy reported that "while the basic ration distribution process is working well, we seem to be running out of food. We have done the maths and there seems to be a shortfall at the end of the distribution cycle. What's more, there are large supplies of food items on sale in the market. Not all of it can be food bartered to complement the diet."

"Well, the reason is clear," Kofi said. "Remember the ration cards I shared with you yesterday. It was pretty obvious they were forgeries. We need to replace them. Tomorrow is the distribution day for the Ethiopian families. I am sure there are single students and ex-combatants amongst them. I propose that we scrutinise the cards more carefully and validate family size. There are five distribution queues. We need five UNHCR staff to monitor each queue."

So, it was decided and Varsha along with Massimo, Mercy, Kennedy and Kofi, would join the distribution. From nine o'clock the next day, each stood beside the local staff employed by the WFP to distribute the rations. Declan also came to observe.

The distribution centre, in a fenced compound, was a timber framed structure with open sides. The roof comprised UNHCR blue plastic sheeting providing simultaneously a modicum of shade and a surfeit of generated heat. A guard at the gate allowed each single refugee or head of household to enter when a distribution slot became available. The refugee showed the ration card, took the food rations, in buckets or bottles, according to the number of family members on the card. They then passed out the back of the shelter. Families waited there to help or young men with home-made wheelbarrows were available for a small fee.

At ten o'clock, a young man approached Varsha's distribution channel. He handed his card to the person checking. Varsha looked over his shoulder. Something was not right. She took the card. The name on the card was Tafesse Barentu, and according to the card he had a wife and five children. It did not take Varsha long to spot the forgery. She called Declan over.

"We should confiscate the card," Varsha said.

Declan smiled. "Let's go and meet his wife and children."

Varsha did not know what he had in mind, but it was not her place to question her boss, especially after just three days at Walda.

"Give him his wheat ration," Declan said to the distribution officer. Tafesse was given a 20 kilo sack of wheat flour. "We will come with you to meet your family," he said. Tafesse struggled to fully comprehend the English but realised he was about to get an escort. He called over a boy with a barrow, but Declan would have none of it. "You can carry it on your shoulders. You are strong enough." Declan indicated in sign language what was expected of Tafesse. On leaving the distribution centre, the heavy sack perched precariously on his shoulders, clearly struggling with the weight in the heat, Tafesse did not turn left to the ex-combatants' section but right to the families' section. Varsha followed. The walk to that section of the camp was short but, once there, Tafesse seemed to be lost. He walked in circles until he found an empty stick shelter and in vain tried to convince Declan that the uninhabited shelter, clearly an outdoor cooking area, was his and his family's. Declan said nothing, just indicated that Tafesse, having relieved himself of the weight of the sack, should place it back on his shoulders and return it from whence it came. Declan was clearly making a point, but Varsha was embarrassed about Tafesse's humiliation. Tafesse's ration card was confiscated and he was asked to re-register and get a replacement card. Declan instructed the food distribution manager that they should no longer accept the old cards. If refugees had old cards they were to be exchanged for the new cards and their family size would be verified.

That afternoon, sitting in the shade, on the veranda of her tent, Varsha could not concentrate on Katharine Hepburn. She realised she had read the last paragraph three times. Her mind was elsewhere, it drifted off the page. Hepburn's image was replaced by Tafesse's. She considered Declan a caring person, who chose, however, to set an example. Yet the refugees were the victims here. Yes, Tafesse cheated and indeed, under normal circumstances, would be punished as a thief. But these were not normal circumstances. Varsha wondered what she might have done, given the opportunity - probably the same. For sure she could not have carried the sack of flour on her shoulders.

Varsha remained at Walda for just under a year. The market grew in size and the refugee camp had quickly taken on the character of a small town. One bore hole produced enough water to reduce water trucking. Sanitation had improved and the death rate had fallen to acceptable levels. All ration cards had been replaced, and food wastage with it. Health centres were meeting the immediate health needs of the population and schools were functioning as best they could. Many refugees were employed by the agencies and paid a small stipend. A few refugees went home, but the camp size had stabilised. Just as things were becoming acceptable, as much as is possible for a refugee camp in the middle of a barren wasteland, it was decided to close the camp and consolidate the Waldan refugees into other camps. Walda, in spite of the improvements, was unsustainable.

After 11 taxing months, Varsha was pleased to get back on the plane for the last time, and through the window of the Beechcraft, as the pilot deliberately circled the remnants of the camp a few times, she reflected on the point of it all. Conditions in the camp had indeed improved. The death rate dropped, security improved, a vibrant soccer league flourished, and children were attending school. There were no longer any defecation fields, but her latrines and her water points were abandoned. The razed land could be returned to the wild animals and to the grazers of cattle and camels who would await the regeneration of the scrub. Walda, once a place where 50,000 souls sat in hope, had come and gone in the blink of history's eye. Varsha believed that she, with her own small effort did good, yet there was now no physical manifestation of any of her achievements. Varsha looked down upon the remnants of Walda, closed her eyes as the plane headed for Nairobi and, as she dozed, wondered where her next assignment might take her.

Guya Goba Bule was still sitting in the shade of his house. The new moon had come and gone 14 times since the camp was born. The refugees had now all been moved. He watched as big lorries hauled away tents, plastic sheeting, large white warehouse tents, water bladders, and leftover supplies. The big white cars, with logos and names in blue on the doors left in convoys. A plane landed on the strip and the nice young lady with brown skin whom he remembered arriving, boarded the plane.

A bulldozer came and flattened the camp. There were no trees nor scrub left, just a barren desert. If the rains came it would be lush and green again in a matter of days. The only thing standing was a hand pump where the big machine had drilled a hole. He slowly got up and wandered over to it and pushed the lever a few times and water flowed. They came, they went, they left behind a water tap, a large pile of discarded timber and a football field. They left the goal posts standing. The hamlet of Walda returned to how it once was and Guya Goba Bule returned to his house to sit in the shade.

He realised, that which had been his daily entertainment – the arrival of the afternoon plane – would be no more. But, whatever he was thinking, could not be discerned from his blank resigned expression.

The Promised Land

Samir shivers. He pulls the meagre blanket he had been given by a well-meaning passer-by over his head and tries to sleep. The park bench is too hard, and, in any case, he is used to sleeping on the bare floor. So, he lies down under the bench, thinking erroneously that it would afford him more shelter. It is not the hard worn patch of grass, but the January cold, that prevents him from sleeping. Well, there is that, and the fact that the police do not take too kindly to too many people sleeping rough in Levinsky Park. Tonight, there is just himself, Rashad and two Eritreans in the square. During the day there are many more, just biding their time, unable to work legally, and whose future might, in all likelihood, be as miserable as their past. Samir hopes that he can get through this night without a visit from the police and, tomorrow, find a room in which to squat. It is just his second night in Tel Aviv and if he does not sort out his permit soon, he fears he will be taken into detention.

Meanwhile, Shoshana is sleeping comfortably (it's all relative), in a small apartment, just some blocks away on Sderot Washington. Now that is a misnomer if ever there was one. Washington "Boulevard" in South Tel Aviv is a lane,

203

much narrower than the surrounding streets, which themselves are shabby and impoverished. Ben Gurion and Rothschild, now they have impressive boulevards in more salubrious parts of town. Even Lincoln has a street of some substance. Does not Washington deserve more than a lane no longer and half the width of a 100-metre athletic track?

Shoshana's apartment, just above a café selling felafel, the smell of stale oil all pervasive, consists of a cramped kitchen with just space for a tiny table and three stools; two small bedrooms, one for her and the other, with a bunk bed, for Uri and Irit; and a bathroom, the shower affording no room for a curtain, so that the floor, the toilet and the basin are wet much of the time. If they did own a proverbial cat, it certainly could not be swung in there.

Each morning, Shoshana prepares breakfast for the children and gets them ready for school. "*Latkas* for breakfast again!" Uri says. "And out of a packet. *Ima*, why can't we have pancakes or eggs? Osem makes pancake mix too in case you are lazy." "I'm not lazy, Uri. I'm always busy and tired, but not lazy. Ok, I will make eggs tomorrow, I promise. You know that I am always running late in the mornings and I need to open the stall on time. When you are finished get your bags. Irit, did you hear me? Put that blasted phone down and get ready."

They exit Washington and turn right into Shalma Road, as usual humming with the morning rush-hour traffic. Shoshana stops in at Ringelblum's and buys two bagels with turkey, tomato and lettuce for the children's lunch, and after 20 minutes she drops them at school. She greats Shmulik, the guard at the gate, with a nod, kisses Uri and Irit and rushes off to open her stall. Shoshana takes the shortcut through the central bus station shopping mall. It has as much charm as a concrete underground car park. Many of the shops in the mall have their shutters drawn and display for-rent signs. The smell of diesel fumes lingers. Shoshana says to herself, again, "God willing, I will soon move out of this wretched place," knowing full well that God is unlikely to oblige. She passes Levinsky Park, frowns, curses and says out loud: "Bloody refugees." Shoshana gets to her stall in the market, raises the shutters and takes the racks of key rings, magnets, scarves, tea towels, baseball caps and other *chachkas* and places them on the pavement. Some locals might buy a gift for a friend, the odd visitor walking from the bus station to town might stop and buy a souvenir, but most are in a hurry and mumble, "I'll buy something on the way back." She remembers them. They never do stop on the way back, just stare at the pavement or cross the road to the other side to pass. Business is bad, and she can hardly pay the rent.

Samir was born in Al Fashir, the capital city of North Darfur. His father, Ibrahim, owned a stall selling woven baskets, which he bought from cattle herders when they came to the market in town. The stall was a simple shelter, a woven rattan mat on the ground covering the red clay patch outside the wall of his house. Another mat, providing some shade from the oppressive heat, was propped up by four crooked wooden poles. On those days when the meagre rains did come in July and August, Ibrahim dismantled the shelter and closed shop. The house behind the wall sat in a small compound. It comprised just one large room made from adobe blocks, the white-washed plaster showing its wear, which Ibrahim could not afford to repair nor repaint. In the corner there was a cooking place and at night Ibrahim rolled out some thin kapok mattresses for himself, his wife and their three children.

Samir and his sisters went to school up to the age of 13 years. They sat on wooden benches, writing in their tatty, dog-eared notebooks whatever the teacher wrote on the faded and pockmarked blackboard. There were a few textbooks, donated by an aid agency, which the pupils shared. On Friday, Ibrahim and Samir, dressed in their white *djellabas*, went to the nearby mosque for evening prayers and on Saturday Samir went to the *khalwa*, the Islamic school, and learned to memorise the Koran, which, if not word perfect, resulted in a beating from the Sheikh.

Darfur had always been neglected by the government in Khartoum, and it was worse since the dictatorship. Al Fashir had grown from a small desert town to a sprawling city of small huts around the now inadequate oasis at its hub. The competition for land between the farmers and the herders provided a constant undercurrent of unrest. The only investment from the government was a massive airstrip. Few locals could afford to buy an air ticket.

When Samir was 16 years old, his cousin appeared at his house. "Samir, come with me and my friends."

"Where are we going, who are these people, why are they carrying guns?"

"Don't ask so many questions Samir. You are about to experience the most important event of your life."

Samir followed blindly. They crossed Al Fashir to the western outskirts and approached the airport. Night had fallen. A dilapidated fence surrounded the runway. This band of some 20 youths entered through a break in the fence and skirted the runway to a hangar which housed fighter jets belonging to the Air Force. While they were laying explosives they were challenged by some soldiers. Samir's cousin and one other amongst their group were wounded, while for the soldiers, the gunfire was fatal. The planes were destroyed and, those whom later the Sudanese government called "rebels", fled to safety. Samir's cousin recovered and what he had called "the most important event in Samir's life" transpired to be no understatement.

Within a few months there was an all-out civil war: Herders against pastoralists; Arabs against non-Arabs; Moslems against Moslems. The massacres, perpetrated by the

206

government proxies, were brutal. Ibrahim's shop was ransacked, one of Samir's sisters was raped in front of her parents and became a mere shell of her lively self, and several boys, in the neighbourhood, not yet teenagers, were abducted to become child soldiers. Samir and his family left their home with the small amount they could carry and walked west to cross the border, to a refugee camp in Chad. The journey took four days in 40-degree heat. On day three, Samir's mother died from dehydration, and a lack of will to see out her life to a more natural end.

Samir and his family were safe, but this was no life. He, his father and sisters shared a tent with another family. The heat inside the tent was unbearable, the mosquitos vicious. Malaria was almost a *rite de passage*, albeit lacking in the celebratory element. Once a week, Samir and his father would go to the food distribution centre and receive a handout of wheat, oil, beans, and, measured in grams, sugar, tea and salt. Just sufficient, carefully calculated calories, to survive. They combined their rations with the others in the tent and sometimes traded a small excess for some meat or vegetables in the market. Ibrahim could not find any work and became increasingly depressed. Samir helped out occasionally doing odd jobs in the health clinic. He was well liked, worked hard and earned a small stipend. There was a football game every evening on a patch of dust behind the market. While affording only a semblance of protection, after dark they retreated into their tents, while the nocturnal criminal elements roamed.

Samir's 17th birthday passed, then his 18th, his 19th, his 20th. Just after he turned 21, he was approached in the sprawling camp market by four men who "suggested" he might like to join the liberation movement and return to Sudan. They would come for him the next day so he could join them in the "noble fight for justice and equality". Samir went home and told his father, who agreed he should flee with the few life savings they could muster. So, at 21 years old, after a tearful parting, Samir walked, begged lifts with truck drivers, took aging buses and crossed Chad, entered back into Sudan further north via Khartoum, on to Cairo, a journey which took six weeks. He found some work for a week in Khartoum on a construction site and the same in Cairo, to earn enough to eat. Samir slept rough on the streets, construction sites and in shop doorways, forever fearful that he would be robbed, kidnapped or abused. He knew he had no future in Chad, Sudan nor even Egypt. He was told by fellow travellers that he would be safe and could claim asylum in Israel.

If he could get to Israel, the Promised Land (well, maybe not promised to him), he believed he would finally find safety and peace. Through the street network it was not difficult to get directions. He took a three-hour local bus ride to Ismailia, for the equivalent of three dollars. After a short walk to the port, the boat trip across the canal on the car ferry took 10 minutes.

He had been warned. "Take care. There are smugglers and traffickers amongst the Bedouin. Some will help you to get to an unguarded border crossing; others will kidnap you for ransom or for slave labour."

"How can I tell the difference?"

"You can't, it is just chance and the will of Allah that will determine your fate."

On the landing, as was expected, his black complexion, meagre belongings and tatty clothes attracted the smugglers. "Do you want to go to Israel? I can take you there. I know the way through the desert and the best place to cross. I have a four-wheel drive. I leave within an hour and you will be there before nightfall, but you should cross after dark. 1,000 dollars."

"I cannot pay that much. I only have 300 dollars left."

The Bedouin smiled. "You are lucky, I already have three passengers waiting in the car. 300 will be okay, but do not tell the others what you paid, otherwise you will regret it.

Understand?"

So it was agreed, with some trepidation. *How do you distinguish a smuggler from a trafficker?*

There were indeed three people waiting in the back of an old single cab Land Rover. The tray, covered by a tarpaulin, open at the rear, had two benches. He climbed in and nodded to his new fellow travellers. The Sudanese man next to him was Rashad from South Darfur. He had tried to claim asylum in Egypt, but the wait was too long and the living conditions harsh, so he decided to take his chances in Israel. Facing them was Dawit, a young Eritrean man and his obviously pregnant wife, Rahwa. Dawit had deserted from the slave-like conditions in the Eritrean army. The four were now in the hands of fate, but today good fortune and Allah shone upon them. The journey was uncomfortable. The driver avoided main roads, the dust cloud behind the vehicle penetrating the place where they sat. Samir and the others covered their faces with scarves, their parched mouths made worse from the dust. They bounced in ruts, swerved around boulders, slid on gravel. Rahwa was clearly in much discomfort, her knuckles white from gripping the seat. Five hours passed, and late afternoon was approaching. The driver stopped in a *wadi,* and they rested against the cliff wall in the shade from the waning sun. If not for the fear and discomfort, the spectacular moon-like terrain may have been cause for some enjoyment.

Their guide took Samir and Rashad up the short but steep incline to the top of the ravine. He pointed out the direction to walk. "From here the way is flat. When it gets dark you will be able to see the lights of a settlement in the distance. Walk towards it. The settlement is on the other side of the border. Usually there are no Israeli border police. If you see someone with a gun they are probably from the Israeli settlement. Good luck. Now I must leave."

They set out just before nightfall to get a head start. All went well and the lights were now just 200 metres ahead.

Suddenly they heard shots, not coming from Israel but from the Egyptian side. Someone shouted in Arabic: "Stop. Egyptian police. If you move we will shoot." Rashad said, "We must run. We are so close." They ran. Dawit and Rahwa lagged a bit behind, the woman clearly struggling. The shooting began again. There was a scream. Rahwa was hit in the leg. Dawit struggled as best he could and Samir doubled back to help and they supported her, limping, towards the lights. Four men appeared in front of them with guns and miraculously the shooting behind ceased. They were in Israel, but, more guns? One man smiled and said in Arabic and English, "You are safe with us. We will help you." Rahwa's wound was superficial and they patched her up. They rested and after three days were given a lift to Tel Aviv. The promised land after all?

It has been said, no idea by whom, that "you are your past", and so it would appear to be the case with Shoshana. Jews are obsessed with their history and ancestry. Not to relate here a genealogy that goes back a century or two, 1930s Europe was a time which defined Israel and Shoshana in equal measure.

Shoshana's grandparents were migrants to Israel. Her grandmother survived the Gross-Rosen concentration camp and fled west after the war to a displaced persons camp in Bavaria. She migrated to Haifa in 1950. Shoshana's grandfather migrated from Yemen in 1951 and her grandparents married soon thereafter. He opened a small jeweller's shop. They had one child. Shoshana's mother, Noa, married Yossi, a third generation *Sabra*. They met while doing military service. She was 19 and he 20 when they married. Shoshana was born a year later after her mother was demobilised. Yossi had aspirations to become an engineer and remained in the army where he could already begin his training in the Israeli Combat Engineering Corps. In October 1973 he was called up to defend his country and was despatched with his battalion to Sinai and, after fierce battles as they approached the canal, Yossi was fatally wounded. Noa was a single mother at 22 and Shoshana was to grow up without a father. After Yossi lost his life, and with a small army pension, Noa wanted to start afresh and decided to try her luck in Tel Aviv. She regretted that move, realising that while part of Tel Aviv was classy, charming and vibrant, South Tel Aviv, to which she moved, was more depressing than the worst parts of Haifa.

Noa struggled to make a living. She helped clean houses and worked as a shop assistant and eventually saved enough to buy a small stall in the market. After leaving school, Shoshana took over her mother's shop. She married at 18 and after she gave birth to Irit and Uri, her husband simply left her without warning and Shoshana was left alone. She was angry and bitter about her lot and wondered why she could not escape the cycle of poverty.

Samir wakes up at first light after a restless night under his bench. He has no idea what to do next. A stranger in a very strange land. Samir asks Rashad. He has no idea either. They ask one of the Eritreans, who thankfully point them in the right direction. "You need to go to the United Nations Office in HaHashmonaim Street. Come, see that tall, modern glass building in the distance over there? There is a shopping mall underneath, go through it and cross the road to an old, long building and look for a sign which says UNHCR. They will help."

Samir and Rashad walk through the mall, self-conscious about their shabby appearance. Shops which they have never imagined, let alone ever seen, flank the wide, neat passages. There is music. The locals look like fashion models. This is a far cry from South Tel Aviv, and Darfur is an age and continent away. The signs are in Hebrew and English, but they can always spot an Arab-looking person and ask directions. They find the office and recognise the UNHCR logo. They have seen it before in Chad and Darfur, on that ubiquitous blue plastic sheeting. Ibrahim had found some in a market stall in Al Fashir and used it to cover the hole in the roof of their house. Something familiar. There are about 30 people in the waiting room. Five small children play with some toys in the corner of the room, Eritreans and Sudanese together. Their mothers are taking the opportunity to catch up on some sleep, albeit uncomfortably on the hard plastic chairs.

After three hours, a welcoming lady who speaks Hebrew, English and Arabic takes their details and gives them a UN registration card. "Tomorrow morning go to the Immigration Office in Lod before nine in the morning. They will give you a temporary resident permit. You will not be able to work, legally," she smiles, or is it a wink? "Today you should go to the African Refugee Organisation just near Levinsky Park. Here is the address. They will find you a place to sleep, give you some money and explain how to get to Lod."

Samir and Rashad spend that night in a run-down hostel, eight to a room, a mix of Eritreans and Sudanese. There is no shortage of horror stories of the journeys and the reception in Israel. Some had spent days in the Holot Detention Centre in the Negev. A few work illegally washing dishes or on constr-uction sites.

Early the next day Rashad and Samir take a bus to Lod and follow the directions they have been given. Already, at eight o'clock a long queue has formed outside. At nine, while they are still in the queue, there is shouting further back.

"What's going on?"

An asylum seeker next to them explains. "The queue closes at nine. The people don't want to leave. They probably came all the way from Eilat where they work in the tourist hotels – look, some have young children with them – but they arrived a few minutes late. They will need to take the five-hour bus back and try another time. There is not much compassion here."

Finally, they are admitted to the reception hall. The room is large with rows of plastic bucket seats. They are instructed to sit in the order in which they arrived. Rashad and Samir are in the 12th row of 20. The reception area is hot, a few ineffective wall fans providing minimal breeze. There are four offices behind glass windows with an official wearing a white blouse or shirt which seems to approximate a uniform. There are four police officers sitting at each corner of the room and a man who seems to be in charge pacing the room and instructing the next in line to enter a room as it becomes free. It seems to Samir that his main purpose is to intimidate, his pistol in a holster at his waist symbolising what seems an unnecessary display of authority.

At noon, Samir and Rashad are next in line. The four officials and the pistol-toting man leave for lunch for one hour. The police are replaced and they go to lunch. The asylum seekers sit and wait.

Soon after lunch, Samir is called in. The woman is kind but business-like. Samir gives his details, which takes time as the woman has a long questionnaire. He is photographed and given an identification card. With it, Samir is given a paper, in four languages, explaining that, as an infiltrator, he cannot work, and must live north of Hadera and south of Gadera, the so called "Hadera-Gadera Visa". If he does not leave Tel Aviv in the coming days he will be sent to prison in Holot.

Samir decides to go underground in Tel Aviv. He finds a job working in a restaurant, is well liked by the restaurant owner, finds a small room in South Tel Aviv and hopes that he will not be picked up by the police. And he waits and waits in the hope that he and the other Sudanese might be recognised as refugees and allowed to stay in Israel indefinitely.

There are many people in Israel who object to the

treatment of the refugees and are incensed that the government calls the Sudanese infiltrators. The number of asylum seekers recognised as refugees can be counted on one hand. Most are rejected and the government offers them money and a flight to Rwanda, with whom an agreement has been signed. Samir has come so far, his employer is kind and amongst the choices with which he is presented he chooses to stick it out in Tel Aviv. He even starts learning Hebrew, and after a year is quite proficient. He wonders what Sheikh Yassim in his old *khalwa* would think of him now.

A year after his arrival, a group of politically active asylum seekers, along with a good many Israelis, decide to organise a vigil in Levinsky Park, protesting against the government refugee policy. They are determined to be peaceful. "We are refugees, not infiltrators," "If we go home, we will be killed," "Non-Jews can be refugees too," read their placards. They stand silently for several hours. The media appears. The police also, but they are respectful and stand to the side. Samir is naturally fearful, as he is not permitted to be in Tel Aviv, but he takes comfort in the crowd.

Before long they are confronted with a counter protest. "Infiltrators go home," "Get out of our park," "You don't belong here," "You are stealing our jobs," read their hastily painted placards. The crowd is angry, slinging insults. At the front of the crowd stands Shoshana. Her life is a struggle and she feels threatened by the arrival on her turf of "these people".

Shoshana comes forward. She is not aggressive, but clearly distraught. Next to Samir stands Yair, a volunteer with the African Refugee Organisation. He whispers to Samir. "You will speak to her in Hebrew and show your human face. Let's see what's on her mind." They step forward to meet Shoshana face to face.

Shoshana is aggressive at first. "You have no right to protest. You have no right to be in our park. You have no right to be in our country. And you," she says, looking at Yair, "how can you, an Israeli, support these people?"

Yair is calm, "I understand what you are feeling,"

"You have no idea what I am feeling. How dare you? I have struggled all my life and suddenly these people come. They are not supposed to work, yet I see them on the construction sites, in the restaurants and the hotels. They came here for a better life. They should fix their own countries and not contaminate ours. What's more, they are Islamic extremists, infiltrators and a danger to the security of Israel!"

It is clear to Yair which newspapers Shoshana reads. Here, in Levinsky Park, is a perfect reflection of the fissure in Israeli society, in Israeli politics. She is repeating the arguments of a certain sector of the media and government proclamations whose messages have fallen on fertile ears. Yair works directly with the asylum seekers, he reads *Haaretz*, not *Yisrael Hayom*. The chasm between these two is unlikely to be solved by confrontation nor probably even by dialogue, in the middle of a park, with the two sides in a face-off.

"Thank you," Yair says. "I think I understand you better. This is Samir. He is from Sudan. Let him tell you his story." Samir had rehearsed his story in Hebrew many times, in Hebrew class, in his mind while washing dishes in the restaurant and in his dreams. A Sudanese Moslem dreaming in Hebrew. His Hebrew is not perfect, but he and Yair can see from her expression that Shoshana is taken aback to be addressed this way. He explains the rape of his sister, the death of his mother, five years in a refugee camp in Chad, the dangers on the route to Sinai, being shot at by Egyptian police and his treatment in Israel. "I have nowhere to go. If I go back, I will be killed." And then the line in the imaginary dialogue he has rehearsed over and over again in his mind's conversation. "How, can you, a country founded by refugees, fleeing tyranny, hate and discrimination, not give us the refuge you were denied? Does not your Bible say 'Love thy neighbour as thyself'. I am your neighbour. Surely Jews, of all people, should be more compassionate? You Jews have a responsibility, not only for your own welfare, but for the world at large."

Shoshana struggles to find an answer. She finds Samir engaging. From afar, sleeping under a park bench, he is a dirty, homeless, dangerous object, a threat to her way of life, her livelihood. But here before her is a calm, kind, clean person, who had made an effort to speak Hebrew and who quotes to her, her Bible. She is moved. She shakes Samir's hand and goes back home to hug her children.

Yair looks at Samir. "Maybe it is possible to change the world one person at a time."

"Maybe. But, the tide is strong. She left, but there are about one hundred others across the park."

The next day, the headline in *Haaretz* reads:
PEACEFUL PROTEST IN LEVINSKY PARK YESTERDAY. 200 Eritrean and Sudanese asylum seekers were protesting against government policy, which does not afford them the rights to which they are entitled under international law. A counter protest from local residents was held across the park. There were no incidents and both sides dispersed peacefully. On another related development, the Supreme Court ruled on Thursday that the policy of the Government of Israel to freeze asylum seeker savings which have been deposited in Israeli Banks, unless they repatriate, was found to be illegal and the law should be repealed. In spite of some small wins in the courts, the government continues to be resistant to recognise as refugees the Eritrean and Sudanese asylum seekers.

The headline in *Yisrael Hayom* reads:
VIOLENT STANDOFF BETWEEN INFILTRATORS AND RESIDENTS IN SOUTH TEL AVIV. A group of 200 Christian Eritreans and Moslem Sudanese invaded Levinsky Park on

the Shabbat. They were confronted by the local residents, whose lives have been economically and socially disadvantaged by the influx of so many Africans over recent months. These people are a risk to the security of the State of Israel. The Israeli Government should reject all claims for refugee status and send all these people back to Africa.

"This is Good.
This is Really Good"

Somewhere, Anywhere, Everywhere
1980 to 2011

Author's Note

From the outset, to avoid any misunderstanding, I want to make clear that this story is a satire. It was inspired by the novel "People in Glass Houses" by Shirley Hazzard, a book about the "Organisation", published in 1967. Ms Hazzard, who had worked for the United Nations for 10 years, was adept at capturing, albeit with some exaggeration, and no modicum of caustic prose, the foibles of the workings of the United Nations as she saw it in the late '50s and early '60s. I thought a story, using the same tongue-in-cheek style, might be interesting. I am not sure whether Ms Hazzard truly felt as critical of the United Nations of her day, as may be assumed from reading "People in Glass Houses", but I can assure you that while I too, in this story, have reflected on many absurdities, consider any criticism of the United Nations, to which I am by no means blind, are far outweighed by its many achievements as a force for good in this troubled world.

"This is good. This is really good. Well done." Sabine blushed. She was even more chuffed because English was not her mother tongue. What's more, she admired Lunz. He was one of the handful of brains who joined in the '50s. Most of them were war survivors, a few from the camps, or refugees who had managed to get out before the war. Most enunciated the English language in a manner that reminded Sabine of a dictionary falling open. Words which she rarely heard, spewed out, with Oxbridge accents, albeit with roots in Prague, Berlin, Vienna, Lemberg or Lodz. It had that sing, a ring, an occasional lisp. "This is good. This is really good." Coming from Lunz there was a poetic cadence, in spite of the simplicity of the statement. Sabine thought she had done good. It was a mere page and a half of typed notes from a hastily called meeting of member states: the Interim Ad Hoc Sub-Working Group on Operational Effectiveness. They called it interim to appease those who objected to yet another "standing" committee and ad hoc so that those who were not invited to attend were not offended, and operational effectiveness was sufficiently nuanced so that the Sub-WG could deal with the feasible and avoid the controversial without too much criticism.

Sabine had only joined the organisation two years prior, fresh from her postgraduate studies and eager to save the world. Her thesis on "The Pitfalls of Inappropriate External Interventions on Midsize Quasi-Democratic Former Colonies of Ostensibly Benevolent Powers", had been praised by her supervisor and considered a great foundation for a career in an international organisation. Her fluency in French and English was welcomed by the interview panel, although her nationality from an "ostensibly benevolent power" was considered a handicap from the point of view of geographic diversity. In those days, her gender was not a favourable consideration. Indeed her entry level grade was a step lower than Andrew Smithington, a male colleague of the same age with whom she attended what, in her opinion, fell short of its optimistic name, the two-day Comprehensive Orientation Seminar.

Sabine was a diligent worker, considered herself good at drafting, and had a pleasing personality. She was the most junior professional grade officer in FOMS, the Facilitation of Meetings Section, which placed her above the support staff, but a general dogsbody to everyone else, and especially to the rather, no, let's be honest, extremely, autocratic supervisor, Artimedes Ionesco, who was the Chief of FOMS and considered hierarchy the most essential behavioural trait one could exhibit, without which the organisation might simply wither away. After two years, Sabine came to the conclusion, based on her experiences with Mr Ionesco as a role model, that the organisation comprised bad managers and people learning to be bad managers. She later discovered that she may have been a bit harsh in her assessment, but only a bit.

One morning Mr Ionesco called her into his office and gave her a new assignment, which he sold to her as "a valuable learning experience". By then she had learned that this was a euphemism for a menial task. But this time it transpired it was not so menial and indeed she did learn.

"The Standing Committee on Transitional Working Groups," he said, "has decided on the creation of an Ad Hoc Sub-Working Group. Something to do with operations or effectiveness. I have been asked to identify a rapporteur for the meeting. The Director General places great importance on the Sub-WG's outcomes and expects the impact will be quite measurable. You should report to Conference Room XXVI at nine tomorrow and meet with Heinz Lunz, the Chief of Legal and Associated Peripheral Matters Section, who is Secretary to the Sub-Working Group. He will convey to you his expectations."

Actually, the expectations were quite modest. What was required were not verbatim or even summary notes, simply no more than two pages capturing the gist and principal conclusions of the deliberations. The only additional guideline was that any controversial issues or disagreements between member states should not find their way into the document. The meeting started at 10:30, at 12:30 adjourned for lunch, and giving time for the delegates to take lunch in the 12th floor rooftop restaurant, reconvened at 14:30 providing for a marginally longer afternoon session, before wrapping up at 17:00.

Sabine worked hard at home that evening and into the night. She had taken copious notes and it was a challenge to condense it all into less than two pages. By midnight Sabine was most pleased with herself. Just a tad more than one and a half pages. Organisational prose, she thought, of the highest calibre. She had managed to insert one *a priori*, one *de facto* and a couple of *inter alia*'s. The next morning she went to her office early with her handwritten notes. Elvira, who operated one of the six Wang word processors in the organisation had called in sick, so Sabine asked one of the secretaries to type up the report on her IBM Ball Head Selectric typewriter in time for her 11 o'clock meeting with Lunz in his 10th floor office (one with a lake view).

Heinz Lunz was a kind man. He reminded Sabine of her grandfather, what little she could remember of him. Her grandfather was a mathematics professor who, like Lunz, had an amazingly logical mind. Both wore tweed jackets and woollen ties; both looked at her with a pensive grin over the half lenses of their bi-focal spectacles. She suspected Lunz had also been a professor before the war. Lunz read her masterpiece. He read it again. He stopped. He gazed into the air and contemplated. Sabine sat silently watching a great mind at work. "This is good. This is really good," he said. Sabine smiled but remained silent. Lunz now removed his Montblanc fountain pen from his inside jacket pocket, removed the cap and proceeded to edit. He crossed out words, replaced words, rearranged sentences, moved paragraphs, added new sentences in the margin, and filled up the blank space at the bottom of page two with new text, all while connecting original words, sentences and paragraphs with circles and lines. Watching Lunz work, efficiently and speedily, observing the pearly white Montblanc star bobbing up and down, the resulting image reminded Sabine of a board of snakes and ladders she played as a child. No white margin space was left untouched. Small scrawl even occupied the narrow space between lines.

"Have this typed up," Lunz said. "Let's see how it looks." Sabine did so. Her masterpiece, which clearly fell short of expectations, was now only a shadow of its former self. She had to admit that the new text, once disassembled from the page and reconstituted, was the true masterpiece.

"Lunz tells me you did a very good job," Ionesco said, clearly somewhat disappointed, when Sabine crossed him in the corridor the next day.

"Apparently so," she replied.

A promotion was long overdue. Andrew Smithington had been promoted three years earlier. He was clearly on a faster elevator. Sabine was content enough. She had been transferred to the Department of Peaceful Resolution to Unresolved Conflicts and had been there for four years. Eight years in the organisation and still trying to save the world. At least the opportunities to make a global difference were better in DPRUC than in the Facilitation of Meetings Section. However, after four years it seemed that unresolved conflicts were increasing. Her major success was managing the inaugural drafting conference for the Convention on Chronic Containment – the CCC which was more frequently referred to as the Bermuda Convention, due to the location where the drafting group met over a three-week period. So far 21 states said they would ratify the Convention, none of which were participating in unresolved conflicts. Sabine was praised for her work on the drafting conference by the Brazilian Ambassador da Costa who was the presiding chairman of the conference and who apparently did not hold it against her that she rejected his numerous invitations to dinner in his hotel in Bermuda. Da Costa had obviously mentioned Sabine to the DG, who mentioned her to the Chief of DPRUC, who said she clearly deserved a promotion. The following year, the Promotions Board failed to include her name on the promotions list. Time to move on.

Sabine figured that she might have more responsibility and authority in a field office, possibly a better chance of recognition, and consequently, what she considered, was a well-earned promotion. Rather than choosing a job and a duty station she thought was a good fit, she asked some trusted and experienced colleagues whom they considered to be fair and sympathetic heads of field office. There were two candidates: Majorie Joergensen in Banjul and Solange Martineau in Bangkok. It did not go unnoticed to Sabine that these reputed good managers were two of the very few female heads of office. The Gambia was a tiny programme. It had the advantage that Sabine would be the only other international professional official beside the head of office, so effectively the deputy. This would look good on her CV. Deputy Head of Office did have a nice ring to it. There was a risk however. What if Gambia was, as had been mooted, merged and subsumed by the Senegal field office? Then she would unexpectedly have a new boss, undermining her personal sanity and effectiveness strategy. She decided to rule that out.

Now, Bangkok however was another kettle of Tom Yam. This was a major operation with some 20 professional staff and twice as many locally recruited support staff. She would, if appointed to the vacancy that had become available, be the chief of the Critical Projections and Solutions Section. CPSS was considered a pivotal section in the Bangkok office, requiring liaison with sister agencies in Thailand, with the office of the Director General and other sections at Headquarters including the New Initiatives and Obscure Proposals Section, to which Sabine had an indirect reporting line.

Sabine was both impressed and ashamed of herself. Was she beginning to behave and act in a mercenary manner like one of "them". Was she turning into an Andrew Smithington, working his way up the organisation with strategic scheming, calculating his own trajectory by pleasing his bosses and not putting the organisation first? Surely not. She was better than that. She was in the habit of going home each evening and asking herself, "did I earn my salary today?" She still felt that she did, and was committed to resigning if the answer was no.

Sabine spent her evenings reading management guides, her favourite: "The Dummies Guide to Being a Competent Manager". She discovered that by simply showing a great deal of humility and treating her staff with kindness, they performed well. It was not so hard. *"Oh, Ionesco, you really had no clue."* Apart from managing her team, she discovered that her main job was to write position papers, construct project proposals and report to headquarters. If she were to be honest with herself, CPSS didn't actually achieve anything. Yes they were efficient. Yes they praised themselves for being an exemplary team. But their projections did not lead to any measurable solutions. Sabine did, however, improve her drafting skills.

Solange, her boss, was pleased with Sabine's work. She said so when they met once a year for the annual PRS, the Performance Review Session. Solange ticked the "above expectations" option on all the boxes: punctuality, proficiency, supervision, output, team worker, drafting and so on. It reminded Sabine of the reports she received at secondary school. Solange never wrote any narrative comments, as these were optional. The performance session took no more than 15 minutes and consisted of questions such as "How have you settled?" "Are you managing in the heat?" "How do you like the food in the canteen?" Then Solange got up from her desk, told Sabine that she was doing very well and to carry on in the same manner. In some ways Sabine was pleased that the PRS was brief as she invariably had an urgent pending report to complete for Headquarters.

Sabine hoped that the new position in CPSS would hone her management skills. She now supervised eight staff. Nobody in the organisation was trained to be a manager, it is generally thrust upon the unsuspecting employee. Sabine was rather apprehensive at first, but she fared well. She had had Ionesco as a negative role model. Ironically, that helped. As for Solange, while Sabine was never stressed, and cherished the independence entrusted to her, in retrospect she realised that too much hands-off, and the lack of professional support and direction, was rather unhelpful. She learned lessons from Solange's management style too.

Sabine felt her promotion was long overdue when it did come after three years in Bangkok. She was well behind what she now called the "Smithington Benchmark". However, she knew by now that patience, if not a virtue, would pay dividends in the end. She had come across a few Smithingtons since she joined the organisation. They were pushy, had the gift of the gab, conveyed an aura of efficiency and competence, and at times, to her chagrin, the female ones at least, were ready to provide sexual favours to their bosses. It took a while, but eventually their incompetence was exposed and the promotional elevator started to creak and slow down. This gave Sabine renewed faith in the organisation, but nevertheless left a sour taste which required some sleepless nights to dispel.

As can be deduced from her Smithington Benchmark concept, Sabine was apt to coin phrases or develop concepts for her personal intellectual consumption. One such concept was the PDS – the Personal Dialogue Syndrome. This she experienced when she lay awake at night and had imaginary dialogues with her boss or a colleague. During the dialogue Sabine exhibited a blunt confidence, to speak her mind with fluency, to have a quick comeback to any aggressive retort, to be on the offensive (yet never be offensive), and ultimately "win" the dialogue. With Solange, she had never had such a dialogue, for when they did communicate it was always cordial. She slept well in Bangkok, if the heat did not keep her awake. The PDS was generally deployed with toxic bosses. When she worked for Ionesco, she had a PDS experience practically every night and if ever she had the opportunity to replicate it in real life, it never turned out as rehearsed. She never "won". Sometimes she found herself PDS dialoguing with Smithington, challenging him on his work ethic. Needless to say, she never had the courage to do so in real life. Anyway, he was now back at Headquarters as the *Chef de Cabinet* to the Director General. She wondered if the DG would one day tweak to Smithington's incompetence.

After four years in Bangkok, "critically projecting" yet struggling to "find solutions", it was time to move on. One skill that she was confident she had now mastered was her drafting skill. After all she had had much practice: annual, bi-annual, tri-annual and quarterly reports to Headquarters, situation reports, funding submissions, budget plans, needs assessments, project effectiveness reviews and reports to donors. Luckily, she now had a desktop computer, which while making report writing more efficient, had the perverse effect of encouraging Headquarters to ask for more reports.

Where to now? Calculate the career trajectory or go where the grass might be greener? Sabine tried for both simultaneously. No more desk work if she could help it and time to be her own boss. A position was available as Head of Office in Benin and this seemed to be an astute move. She would be in charge; albeit it of a small office and serving in a Francophone country. That made sense in terms of broadening her experience. Indeed, she was the only contender for the position who spoke fluent French, so that clinched it for her. Her colleagues arranged a farewell party in the cafeteria, Solange made a nice speech and she was presented with a memento of Bangkok: "101 Thai Dishes You Need to Cook Before You Die", which she accepted with a warm smile (wondering if green curry paste or lemon grass would be available in Cotonou).

Sabine returned to Headquarters for a week of de-briefing and briefing. She had a full programme, Monday and Tuesday organised by the Asia Bureau, Wednesday free for admin stuff and meeting the Personnel Section and the last two days organised by the Africa Bureau.

On Wednesday, while sitting alone for lunch in the cafeteria, who should appear but Andrew Smithington. She had supposed that an encounter with him was to be inevitable, and Sabine had mixed feelings. She was somewhat ashamed that she had not progressed in the organisation as speedily as Andrew, but she was nevertheless curious as to how he was getting on in his exalted position as Chef de Cabinet.

"Sabine, what a pleasant surprise. How long has it been now? The Orientation Seminar? That cannot be. How are you? May I join you?"

"Yes by all means Andrew. Nice to see you too. Please join me."

"What are you doing here?"

"I just completed my assignment in Bangkok and am about to take up a new post in Benin as Head of Office." Sabine felt a little cheeky mentioning that she was to be Head of Office. The lack of modesty was, for her, stooping somewhat low, and she should not have felt inferior to Andrew. She was angry with herself.

"Well done." Sabine found his retort had a touch of condescension. "As I am sure you know, I am working with the DG. Most challenging, but exciting, and I dare say a privilege, to be in the centre of the action. I expect I too will be the Head of an Office on my next rotation. I'm thinking of

London or Washington. I believe I am more suited to political offices rather than operational offices in the field. I guess I shall move once the DG's term ends in December."

"Well done." Sabine hoped she sounded adequately insincere.

It was an uncomfortable lunch and as soon as she had finished eating, Sabine excused herself, saying that she needed to go to the medical unit to get her vaccinations, which was partially true as the appointment was much later in the day.

Her briefing schedule included Artimedes Ionesco who was now the Director of the Bureau for Africa. It was essentially a courtesy call as all new Heads of Offices met the Director. Ionesco was charming, as though he and Sabine were long lost friends. Sabine remained courteous, after all it was a courtesy call. It was from him that Sabine was upset to learn that Heinz Lunz, her "snakes and ladders" role model as she personally referred to him, and who had retired soon after they had ever so briefly worked together, had passed away. He must have been about 75 years old, but he had had a hard life during the war, probably in a concentration camp. Some said it was surprising he lived as long as he did. Sabine was sure it was because he had such an active mind, which compensated for a frail body. Although she encountered Lunz ever so briefly, she now realised what a substantial impression he had made on her. After leaving Ionesco's office, Sabine went outside, sat by the lake under a willow tree and wept. It seemed appropriate.

After her week at Headquarters, Sabine left for Benin transiting Paris. She was met at Cotonou airport by Utete, a young man who was to be her driver. But he was more than that. Utete was the "fix it" person at the office. He was adept at manoeuvring new arrivals through the machinations of the airport. Utete knew where to get things – if it was available in Benin, he knew how to get it. He knew customs officials, property agents, police sergeants, local government officials, and were to get West African CFA francs on the "informal" market. In other words, he was the oil that allowed the office to function. And he did so with a broad smile that never seemed to be erased. Sabine and her nine suitcases were whisked through customs and immigration as fast as a franc could grease a palm and she was driven the short distance to the Novotel, her temporary home until she could find an apartment.

In December the Director General's term came to an end. The new DG was an American, Bartholomew Harrington (the third), who had served many years in the US State Department. He was not unlike previous DGs, all of whom felt that what had gone before was mediocre, but, finally, the organisation was fortunate to have a new and experienced captain at the helm. So, in February, after Harrington had settled into his penthouse apartment, not far from the embassy of the United States, he called all staff together and announced FIG, the Framework for Innovative Governance. "This will revolutionise the way we work," he proudly pronounced. "We will work in new ways, have a greater impact in what we do and be recognised as a leading-edge organisation - an example of good governance, for which we can all feel rightly proud."

Five working groups were formed. They were called alpha, beta, gamma, delta and epsilon. No one knew why. But it just sounded more exotic, maybe even more professional, than working groups 1 to 5. They dealt respectively with organ-isational structure; staffing and productivity; finance and resource allocation; impact and accountability; and outreach and field harmonisation. Sabine, who could have done without the "honour", was assigned to WG Epsilon. The Africa Epsilon Sub-WG met in Nairobi three times in that first year of the Deliberations, Design and Development (D^3) phase of FIG. She was not unhappy to get a break from Benin, although for the life of her she could not understand why the Nairobi office arranged for the meetings to take place in the Ascot Hotel, a rather shabby downtown building where it was hard to tell whether the cockroaches outnumbered the prostitutes in the lobby or vice versa. Probably because she was the most junior Head of Office, she was designated Rapporteur and, as a result, in December attended the Epsilon Global WG in Rome. Probably 60% of Sabine's time was taken up with FIG that first year. She drafted (rather well, she thought) copious reports, conclusions and proposals. The whole process was incredibly disruptive. It seemed to her that output and impact suffered rather than improved. As for harmonisation, she did not detect improved coordination, cooperation nor indeed harmony. The estimated cost of FIG was rumoured to be in the region of three million dollars.

In February, Bartholomew Harrington proudly declared that the first D^3 phase of FIG was an outstanding success and announced the creation of two FIG Implementation Units: Psi and Omega, one for headquarters and the other for the field. Sabine was spared any involvement in these.

Rather relieved, albeit noticing only marginal improvement in the functioning of the organisation, yet paradoxically an increased number of reporting obligations to Headquarters, Sabine turned her attention to her small domain. She felt empowered. Sabine believed she was a good supervisor and met with her staff four times a year to discuss their performance and give guidance. In these discussions there was no mention of the quality of the food in the food outlet (it did not qualify to be called a restaurant) from which many of the staff bought their lunch to eat at their desks. She hoped that she ran both an efficient and happy office.

In her second year, Sabine participated in drafting the Déclaration d'avancement de l'alignement ambitieux, known in English as The Advancement of Aspirational Alignment Declaration for Francophone West Africa. All the Organisation's Heads of Offices and their government counterparts met in Cinkassé, a small town in the very north of Togo on the border with Burkina Faso, to construct the AAA for Francophone West Africa. Again Sabine was perplexed about the choice of venue. Why was this town, so far from any capital or city of any substance, chosen? She could only assume it was because it was the hometown of the Minister of Development of Togo, who probably also owned the Auberge Central in which the delegates were staying.

The Auberge Central was a 3-star establishment. It was clean, with a small unadorned restaurant and bedrooms equally unadorned. Utilitarian was the best description. On the ground floor there was a room that was set up as a theatre, with 12 rows of seats one would find in a movie theatre. It was totally impractical for a participatory conference. The first order of business was to listen to a point of order from the Minister of Development of Burkina Faso, who was upset that the meeting was not being held in Cinkansé which was no more than a 15-minute walk across the border. After some debate, it was agreed that the final communiqué announcing the AAA Declaration, should it be successfully concluded, could be called the Cinkassé/Cinkansé Conclusions.

It came as no surprise to Sabine that she was nominated to be Rapporteur, a task to which she had now become accustomed. Six days in Cinkassé were six days too many for Sabine and indeed for all the delegates. The lack of comfort was the likely reason that the deliberations proceeded apace, and the AAA Declaration concluded in record time, especially when Sabine compared it with the inordinate amount of time required for the drafting of the Convention on Chronic Containment, which, Sabine recalled fondly, had met in Bermuda, a short walk from the beach. Sabine mused that one thing both Bermuda and Cinkassé had in common was sand. It was decided that any follow up to the AAA Declaration should take place in "more suitable" location.

Sabine liked her time in Benin. Cotonou was not a large city and the capital city, Porto Novo, which she visited frequently, was just a short distance away. There was a small but socially active expatriate community of diplomats, international civil servants and private business folks. Home entertainment was the norm as the number of good restaurants was limited. She worked hard and managed to chalk up some achievements between her reporting obligations to Headquarters. Sabine believed, in her heart that the balance sheet would show that, yes, here she had earned her salary.

One night, Sabine had a dream. She was walking through a rocky desert. She was parched. Her water bottle was leaking. There seemed to be an endless supply of water dripping from the bottle and, as hard as she tried, she could not stop the flow, yet whenever she put the bottle to her lips, the bottle was empty. In the distance, through the heat haze, she saw what appeared to be an oasis. It could have been a mirage. She tried to run but stumbled, could not get up, so she crawled over the rocky terrain and the oasis came closer. Shortly before the oasis, to her left and to her right, she noticed men in suits sitting around conference tables, clearly engaged in matters of high importance. Sabine crawled further. Her knees and hands were bleeding, yet there was no pain. A stand of acacia bushes lay ahead and when she emerged on the other side, there appeared an escalator rising to the sky. She crawled onto the moving steps and pulled herself up to a standing position. Her wounds had healed and she was no longer parched. The desert receded into the distance behind and below her. Ahead of her she could discern a person approaching on the down escalator. As he came closer she recognised him. Andrew Smithington. Blood on his hands, no longer in a dapper suit, white shirt and silk tie, but pyjamas. He did not look at Sabine but simply gazed ahead blankly into the distance. She turned around and watched as she ascended and he descended, until he was but a speck. Sabine was not sure how long she had been on the escalator when she woke up. She lay in bed, perspiring, the ceiling fan generating only a modicum of cool air. She watched its perpetual rotation in the dim light and could not get back to sleep.

Sometime after the beginning of her third year (and six months after her strange dream) two juxtaposed events happened that equally vindicated and perturbed Sabine. She was promoted to a higher grade just as soon as she became eligible, probably due to her high-profile work on FIG. In the same week, she learned through the rumour mill that Andrew Smithington had apparently been accused of sexual harassment by one of his staff. Nothing was definitively proven, but rather than go to the administrative tribunal, and to avoid dismissal, after the intervention of the mediator, Smithington was demoted one grade and assigned to "special duties", a euphemism for parking an embarrassment out of harm's way. Needless to say, the young lady who had made the accusation was only partially satisfied with the outcome.

Sabine had now come to the conclusion that the field was where the action was, and Headquarters was kind of spectator sport. For the next 10 years she had assignments in Iraq and Senegal as Deputy and in Dacca, again as Head of Office. While in Dacca she was promoted again and the stark choice was presented to her – stay in the field or try to make a difference in Headquarters. Would she be a spectator? Sabine hoped not, but it was clear that the organisation expected her to show her face again in Headquarters. It was apparent to her that it was because there was, in Headquarters, a dearth of women in senior positions. The donors were looking at the statistics, and they were found to be wanting. The irony was that Sabine was offered the position of Chief of Facilitation of Meetings Section, in which she served when joining the organisation. She would dearly have liked to turn it down, but it was made clear, in not-so-subtle ways, that it was the wish of the DG and she had to be seen to be a good team player.

Sabine was not happy at all. This was an administrative job which soon became routine. There was no possibility for innovation and it proved to her that Headquarters was not for her. Nevertheless, she worked hard and in addition to facilitating meetings became an active participant in the many Headquarters conferences, working groups, committees, task forces, think tanks and communities of practice.

One such conference was the Interagency and Inter-governmental Conference on Exceptionalism. Sabine was asked to provide a rapporteur for the Conference, for which she offered one of her staff, an intelligent and enthusiastic young man, Geronimo Escudo, who had joined the organ-isation and FOMS just a year earlier. Although Geronimo was Ecuadorian, he had studied at the London School of Econo-mics, from where he graduated with a Masters in Manage-ment and Strategy. Sabine offered to guide Geronimo as this was an important conference and the reputation of FOMS was to some extent on the line. After the first day, Geronimo presented Sabine with a three-page summary of the deliberations. Geronimo sat patiently while Sabine read the summary. Then Sabine, looked up, paused for a good minute, and with all the sincerity she could muster said, "This is good. This is really good. Leave it with me. I might make some minor changes, but it's very good."

Autobiographical Notes

When Your Chickens Come Home to Roost

The United Nations likes systems. It constantly strives for efficiencies of scale. The specialists, in functions such as human resources, finance, procurement, media relations, across all UN agencies meet regularly to streamline procedures. In the '90s nearly all agencies began to explore Enterprise Resource Planning (ERP) systems, mainly in the areas of human resources and finance. While serving as Chief of Staff Development and also as Deputy Director of Human Resources at the UNHCR Headquarters in Geneva, I was intimately involved in the development and implementation of UNHCR's ERP.

In Addis Ababa, as UNHCR Assistant Representative, I oversaw the Finance Unit. From there I made frequent trips to Nairobi. I only once participated in the Hash which departed from the Hilton Hotel every Saturday.

Towards the end of my career and, as a consultant after retirement, I developed and delivered training to UN staff in management and leadership. I worked with the UN System Staff College (UNSSC) very closely for five years while Chief of Staff Development at UNHCR and was, for two years, seconded to the Staff College. Although based in Geneva, I frequently travelled to Turin. The river did flood its banks while I was there, and the Turin gorgonzola and pear pizza is indeed delicious.

Water to Dust
Somalia

I was assigned to Mogadishu, Somalia for two years in 1987 as a UNHCR programme officer responsible for education activities and construction projects for camp-based refugees. In the course of my work, I travelled twice by road to the refugee camps around Luuq. There was something magically beautiful about the desert landscape. The Juba and Shebelle rivers provided some lush vegetation and a respite from the surrounding dry landscapes, which nevertheless had their own charm. The villages through which we passed comprised simple, single story adobe dwellings. On route we passed nomads travelling with their camels, *akal* houses and cattle. Some of the roads were simply a maze of zigzagging dust tracks as described in the story.

I have been flexible in describing the timing of the floods. When assigned to Addis Ababa between 1996 and 1991 there were serious floods in the Dollo region of Ethiopia which also affected the Luuq region of Somalia across the, then submerged, Dollo bridge. With colleagues, I flew into an air-strip near Dollo to undertake a needs assessment of the impact of the floods on refugee populations.

The incident at the Somali checkpoint is based on an actual personal experience, but the personal letter from my mother, which I eventually handed over, was handwritten on one of those, now non-existent, aerogrammes and looked un-mistakably unofficial, yet seemed to do the trick and my driver and I were allowed to pass without money changing hands.

Trying to Make Sense of it all
Hong Kong

I was assigned to the Office of the UNHCR Chief of Mission in Hong Kong from 1989 to 1992 as Assistant Representative for Administration and Assistance Programmes. One of my tasks was to attend the bi-weekly "Accommodation Meet-ings". Their purpose was to identify living space for new arrivals of Indo-Chinese asylum seekers. Much of course was arranged outside these meetings, but this was the one coordination meeting comprising all departments concerned. The government of Hong Kong struggled to find accommodation for the increasing number of new arrivals. The ferries and the airstrip runway were just two of the numerous accommodation options established by the Hong Kong government.

The Voluntary Repatriation Programme to Vietnam run by UNHCR and the International Organisation for Migration (IOM), and the more or less involuntary, so-called Orderly Return Programme run by the government, were both implemented simultaneously. The description of "information" sessions and the self-stabbing incident at Whitehead Detention Centre (which I witnessed) are accurate. The latrines at Shek Kong were constructed as described.

That Voice in My Head
Iraq

After the Iraqi invasion of Kuwait, the northern Iraqi Kurds staged a rebellion, which was brutally crushed by Saddam's army using helicopter gunships. Hundreds of thousands of Kurds fled to Turkey and Iran and in March 1991, once the situation had stabilised, returned in huge numbers. They needed protection, transport, food, non-food items, shelter and health care. Fortunately, the coalition forces along the Turkish border were able to provide a first response, but the needs were urgent and massive. In June 1991, I was asked to temporarily leave my assignment in Hong Kong, to participate in UNHCR's emergency response for refugees returning to Iraq.

I was assigned as Head of the UNHCR Sub-Office in Erbil. We were loaned an office in a house next door to the Governorate. The Governor was a Sunni Arab, loyal to

Saddam Hussein's government.

The main road led east to the Iranian border. After leaving the Erbil plain, the road began to wind up into the mountains, through the most spectacular terrain. Before the town of Shaqlawa there was a checkpoint manned (and womanned) by Kurdish *Peshmurga*. We were now in de facto Kurdish controlled territory.

It was hot in June in Iraq. In Erbil, my colleagues and I, with whom I shared a house, slept on matrasses on the roof in the open air. The temperature inside the houses made it just too uncomfortable to get a good night's sleep in the bedrooms. We were not alone. From our roof we could look across at the roofs of the surrounding houses at our sleeping neighbours.

There was a curious incident at one of the checkpoints. I was driving in a Landcruiser into Kurdish territory. The *Peshmurga* checkpoint guard asked for my ID. I said, "You know me, I come here regularly. Why don't you just wave me through?" He replied, "Yes I know you, but I like it when you wind down the window and I can feel the cool air from your air conditioning."

The characters in this story and their conversations come from my imagination. What was true, was that one day a body was indeed dumped in the front yard of our office. I have no idea why. Then a few days later a massive crowd appeared in front of our office. Some protesters with placards with anti-government slogans appeared, infiltrated the crowd and incited them to protest more aggressively. After a short time, the police and special forces moved in with tear gas. The crowd dispersed and some approached our office property. We did allow them to enter and helped those affected by tear gas to recover. Later I led the small group out the back door to the street at the rear of our office. The incident with the machine gunner on the pick-up truck occurred as described in the story. I have kept that UN armband as a treasured memento. It was only later that one of the local staff, who had

talked to the protesters, said that there had been signs in the
market stating that we would distribute free food on that day
and that it was allegedly some Iranian *agent provocateurs*
who inspired the riot.

Where in Hell is Walda?
Kenya

From 1991 to 1996 I worked out of Geneva in the
Emergency Preparedness and Response Section. One of my
first assignments was a two-month stint in Walda Refugee
Camp. I arrived on the same day as a safari company were
setting up a residential facility for UNHCR staff in the heart of
the camp. I counted myself fortunate that I had not arrived
earlier, as all the staff who had arrived at the onset of the
influx fell ill from the unsatisfactory living conditions. Some
were evacuated with hepatitis. This accentuated the importance of staff having good healthy living conditions if they are
to be effective in helping refugees.

There was indeed a serious issue with forged ration cards,
but this situation was soon corrected and all old ration cards
were replaced with the approved UNHCR identification and
ration cards. Some of the forged cards were imaginative to say
the least. Apart from the mirrored stamps, some were simply
blank cards with lines ruled in red and blue ink to appear like
index cards. I did witness the incident with a refugee carrying
a 20 kg sack of wheat flour on his back to a small shelter which
was clearly not his.

Walda was closed after only 15 months. In March 1993 the
refugees were transferred to Kakuma Refugee Camp and to
three camps: Ifo, Dagahaley and Hagadera, which are
collectively known as Dadaab. These camps still exist today,
30 years after the first influx in 1991. Kakuma houses 180,000
persons and Dadaab Camps 320,000. The population is not

static. Some have repatriated, some have resettled to third countries and there have been waves of new arrivals.

The Promised Land
Israel

From July 2008 to November 2008, I was assigned to Tel Aviv on a temporary basis to head the UNHCR Office. Due to the influx of asylum seekers from Sudan and Eritrea from the end of 2006, the UNHCR staff numbers expanded manyfold. The office faced many challenges ensuring pro-tection for asylum seekers and worked with the Israeli government to ensure adequate refugee status determination procedures were in place. The government made it very difficult for the asylum seekers, placing many obstacles in their way. While Eritreans and Sudanese were granted refugee status at a rate of over 90% worldwide, while Israel only recognised some 1% as refugees. The asylum seekers faced many hardships and the Israeli population was split between those who thought the asylum seekers were infiltrators and should be sent home, and those (including a number of NGOs and academic institutions) which provided considerable support to the asylum seekers. The anti-refugee factions protested publicly from time to time and I witnessed a public protest by Sudanese asylum seekers in the centre of Tel Aviv which concluded peacefully. There are still (2023) some 25,000 Eritrean and Sudanese asylum seekers in Israel, including 8,000 children who were born there.

"This is Good. This is Really Good."

The seed for this story is an event in Geneva during my first position at UNHCR in about 1980. I was a junior staff member and was asked to make a summary of a discussion for a newly created standing committee of the UNHCR governing body, the Executive Committee (EXCOM). I prepared the summary notes and met with a senior director, a gentleman with a brilliant legal mind and a kind heart, who, after praising the text and my effort, proceeded to pull it apart. To this day I regret not having kept the document with its corrections and additions as a memento of a novice's lack of competence and wisdom.

As noted in the preamble to the story, it is highly satirical and, while exaggerated, is based on a number of personal experiences and reflections from my United Nations career.

About the Author

Michael was born in Auckland, New Zealand. He completed a Bachelor of Arts degree at Auckland University in 1972 and joined the Ministry of Foreign Affairs in Wellington. In 1976, Michael spent two years in the Hague where he gained a master's degree in development studies.

In 1979, Michael began working for the United Nations High Commissioner for Refugees (UNHCR). He worked for UNHCR for 32 years in a range of functions and in various locations, including Switzerland, Australia, Somalia, Hong Kong, Ethiopia and Israel. He also spent two years working for the International Labour Organisation and two years with the UN System Staff College. Michael retired from the UN in 2011 and worked for several years as a consultant in management and leadership training. Michael and his wife, Maricela, divide their time between Madrid, Spain and San Miguel de Allende, Mexico.

Previous Books
A family biography *What's Luck Got to Do with It?*
An historical thriller *The Degenerate Saxophonist*

Printed in Great Britain
by Amazon

42820462R00148